1

Benson the Boxer

Program for Loss and Grief

A Manual for Therapists, Educators and Parents working with Children

Written by Karen Ferry

Illustrated by Selinah Bull

Note to Readers: Standards of clinical practice and protocol change over time, and no technique or recommendation is guaranteed to be safe or effective in all circumstances. This manual is intended as a general information resource for professionals practicing in the field of psychotherapy and mental health; it is not a substitute for appropriate training, peer review, and/or clinical supervision. Neither the publisher nor the author can guarantee the complete accuracy, efficacy, or appropriateness of any particular recommendation in every respect.

For information about permission to reproduce content from this book, please write to:
Permissions, CORTXION BrainSmart Enterprises Pty Ltd.
PO Box 242, Upper Beaconsfield, VIC 3808 Australia
Email: cortxion@gmail.com

Neuropsychotherapy advisor - Pieter Rossouw

Cover design by Cameron Ferry (cameron@nyidedesign.com)

Production Manager: Jonathan Wills (talkingtherapy@me.com)

Unless otherwise noted, the illustrations were created by Selinah Bull
(selinah@selinahbull.com)

Title: Benson the Boxer: Program for Loss and Grief
Includes bibliographical references

ISBN : 978-0-6483275-1-6

1. Neuropsychotherapy. 2. Psychotherapy. 3. Brian-based therapy.
4. Neuroscience. 5. Brain research. 6. Brain based workbook. 7. Children's activity workbook. 8. Educational workbook.

BrainSmart Enterprises Pty Ltd. CORTXION
PO Box 242, Upper Beaconsfield, VIC 3808
email: cortxion@gmail.com

Dedication

This book is dedicated to Joshua and Cameron in memory of their boxer dog Benson. It is also dedicated to every child who has ever experienced a situation of trauma and loss, with the hope that there can be healing and a moving forward from the pain they have experienced.

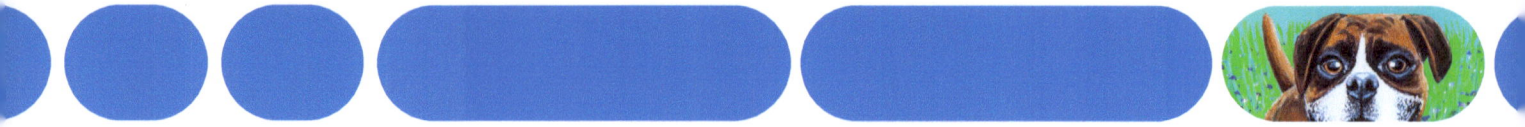

PREFACE

Life is about sharing, experiences, happiness and fun. We all aim for these (and other) qualities. These are also our hopes and dreams for young people. Sadly, there are curve balls in life and unfortunate situations happen. These experiences shape us but can also threaten to derail our trajectories in life.

It is very exciting to introduce "Benson the Boxer – A Story of Loss and Life" to young people. The storybook and associated workbooks aim to guide young people through the distress of life changing events. These resources are developed from a neuroscientific perspective and, as this associated manual explains, are designed for use by parents, carers, teachers, counsellors, and other professionals to guide young people from behavioral patterns of confusion and avoidance to gradual patterns of re-engaging.

Benson is the result of science, of dedication, of passion and a deep sense of care. I would like thank Selinah Bull who has brought the characters in the storybook to life, which I believe will heighten the engagement of young readers and makes these resources all the more valuable for therapeutic interventions.

My deep gratitude goes to so many who provided valuable comments and supported this journey. Special thanks to lecturer Pieter J Rossouw for the insights into neuropsychotherapy and his passionate encouragment for this project. Sincere appreciation to valued friend and advisor, Matthew Dahlitz; copy editor and trusted mentor Jonathan Wills; photographer Aaron Bellette; and my son Cameron Ferry for design and layout. His endurance through this long journey, and the countless hours of labour make these truly special resources.

Karen Ferry

CONTENTS

FOREWORD

Every once in a while you get to read a book (and related resources), that is a total stand out and say: 'Brilliant! Absolutely brilliant!' As an educator, this superbly written and illustrated book provides a powerful resource for not only its intended audience of children and young people, but for all those who work with them to support their wellness as they deal, from time to time, with matters like trauma and grief. It provides invaluable insights on dealing with the problems from such experiences using a fantastic story about two young dogs who are great friends. The authors lead their readers into the mind and lived experiences of Benson, a Boxer, and how initially he unsuccessfully deals with the trauma and misery of losing his closest friend, Lucy who is run over by a truck while they are playing. The story about the accident and its aftermath are very real and children are likely to see themselves in such situations experiencing similar things. The messages will likely have very positive immediate and continuing influences on thinking about and dealing with trauma in ways that allow the sufferer to ultimately move forward and thrive.

A significant part of the brilliance of this book is the use of the latest scientific evidence-based research on the brain to inform it. It is a tall order to produce a very high quality children's book in itself, let alone one incorporating contemporary scientific research. It is likely to have a great positive impact on the wellness of those who use it.

I highly recommend 'Benson the Boxer: A Story of Loss and Life' as an invaluable resource for children and young people and all who work with them in dealing with trauma and grief – and really anything that is bad, sad or scary - and learning how to strongly build wellness. Indeed, it should be essential reading for those working with children and young people in such situations as it gives neuroscientific understandings on working effectively with them to achieve wellness.

Ken Purnell, Professor of Education | School of Education and the Arts,
Central Queensland University, Australia.

SECTION 1:

Brief Overview Of Childhood Loss And Trauma

1.1 DEFINING LOSS, TRAUMA AND STRESSFUL EVENTS

Children experience many situations of loss in the normal developmental stages associated with growing up; for example, giving up a pacifier or a comfort toy.[8] However, children routinely experience more significant losses or compromised environments. Situations such as divorce, parental separation and losses associated with death are common realities for many children.[6] There may also be loss associated with a health issue, an accident, a natural disaster, or a change of home environment, which leaves a child with a loss of identity within a new community.[3,8]

Some children can maintain a relatively stable equilibrium and are able to make healthy adjustments to situations of loss.[3] Others suffer acute distress and adopt trauma related behaviours.[3,6]

A child's response to loss depends on their resiliency, either inherent or learned. Protective factors also include the availability of external sources of support, the child's age and their developmental level.[6] A child's reaction to loss is related to their personal perspective of the loss and the meaning that was attached to the event or object now gone, or the person no longer with them.[6,8]

We ought not to shield children from loss and recognise that most have a certain resilience to be able to work through loss, and the "normal" grieving process, unassisted.[3] However, some children, and adults, suffer acute distress and are unable to recover alone.[3]

Others appear to recover quickly, but they are unable to enjoy life as they used to. They become fearful and anxious over seemingly irrelevant circumstances. They can't focus or concentrate and may experience unexpected health problems.[3]

This *Benson the Boxer* storybook and associated worksheets are devoted to the latter group. The story was developed for children who have been traumatised due to the loss of someone significant in their lives. The term "trauma" when used in this manual, refers to the cognitive, behavioural, emotional and/or physical difficulties that are directly related to the experience of loss.

When a child experiences the loss of a loved one under traumatic circumstances the trauma symptoms may interfere with, and impinge on, the normal grieving process. If left unaddressed, the trauma can result in unresolved grief, leading to serious levels of dysfunction in later years.[6]

Trauma can occur after a severe and/or extroadinary stressor, such as the loss of a caregiver, or a life threatening circumstance, leaving the victim feeling helpless and impairing normal everyday functioning.[18,22] Children are often considered to be highly resilient to stressful and traumatic situations, with many believing that young people "get over things easily". However, neuroscience research suggests children are more vulnerable to trauma than adults.[25] Frightened or traumatised children (particularly young children) do not possess the social, developmental, or psychological maturity to comprehend what has happened to them and commonly express their feelings by means of behavioural changes.[11] If the grief and trauma is not worked through, the emotional impact of the experience may resurface at a later time, often with unanticipated results.[18]

1.2 IMPACT OF LOSS ON CHILDREN

Children perceive situations of loss in unique and diverse ways.[13] While it is recognised that perceptions and reactions to loss will vary according to each individual child, the following guide may be used to assist therapists, teachers and parents in their understanding of the different chronological ages and developmental stages when a child suffers loss.[4,8]

Stage 1: 3-5 years

- Children in this age group are egocentric, lacking cognitive under standing of death and related concepts.
- Death is seen as reversible and not permanent.
- **Common grief response:** It is not uncommon to see developmental regression, such as bed-wetting, changes in eating and sleeping patterns or general irritability.

Stage 2: 5-9 years

- Death is seen as something that happens only to old people
- These children live with fantasy and wishful thinking.
- Death is seen as irreversible, but not inevitable.
- There is a very strong sense of guilt and responsibility
- **Common grief response:** There are many questions of "how" and "why". There is considerable distress and confusion commonly resulting in nightmares and eating problems, violent play or a regression and withdrawal from friends and family.

Stage 3: 10+ years

- Cognitive ability is more developed along with logical and concrete thought processes.
- Death is acknowledged as irreversible and inevitable.
- Children may see death as punishment and have a personal fear of bodily harm.
- These children desire details of events and observe how others respond to death.
- There is an understanding of grief and mourning.
- **Common grief response:** Withdrawal from friends and family is common. Sleep and eating difficulties can develop. Confusion, behaviour difficulties and school problems can emerge.

1.3   TRAUMA ASSOCIATED WITH LOSS

When a child experiences sudden and significant loss, feelings of anxiety, depression, helplessness and guilt are common.[28] Most children experiencing bereavement have an innate resilience and if the child is given the opportunity and time to work through the loss, they eventually are able to resume day-to-day activities.[28]

However, Roberts (2001) asserts that grief and posttraumatic stress reactions are common and can manifest together and interplay between each other, or grief and posttraumatic stress symptoms can occur independently from each other.[28] Stress and fear can result due to the trauma and horror of the event itself,[28] or as a result of the momentous changes and the many transition events that relate to the loss.[8]

When a child experiences the death of a significant person in their life their level of security is shifted, along with familiar, safe relationships, and in many situations, their own sense of identity.[8] There arises a fearful awareness that they (the child) has been unable to protect either themselves or their friend or family members from the realities of death.[28,33]

Based on the typologies of Everstine & Everstine (2013) and Joshi, Lewin & O'Donnell (2005), the following are commonly exhibited responses to stress and trauma in the three major age groups.

Preschool: 2-4 years

- Fear of being alone and excessive clinging
- Regressive behaviour
- Sensitivity to loud noises
- Confusion and irritability
- Aimlessly wandering or running
- Eating and digestion problems

School-age: 5-11 years

- Non-specific physical problems (aches and pains)
- Sleep difficulties (nightmares and trouble falling asleep)
- Eating and digestion problems
- Sadness
- Withdrawal from peers
- Irritability

- Increased fearfulness (fear of loud noises etc.)
- Whining and clingy behaviours
- Aggression towards authority
- School avoidance and loss of interest in normal daily activities
- Difficulty concentrating
- Isolation
- Regressive behaviours (e.g. bed wetting, baby talk, carrying a 'comfort', or a soft toy etc.)
- Guilt and shame with the child believing the traumatic event was their fault, or they could have prevented it from happening

Adolescent: 12+ years

- Non-specific physical problems (aches and pains)
- Appetite changes
- Sleep difficulties (nightmares and trouble falling asleep)
- Sadness
- Withdrawal and preferring isolation
- Irritability
- Excessive worries and fears
- Agitation and apathy
- Risk taking behaviours
- Poor concentration
- Avoidance behaviours
- Disenchantment (what's the point?)
- Feelings of hopelessness and helplessness
- Guilt and shame

1.4   STRESS AND TRAUMA FROM A NEUROSCIENCE PERSPECTIVE

When a child is exposed to a traumatic situation, fear and anxiety becomes a reflexive reaction escalating the "fight" or "flight" response in the autonomic nervous system.[6, 32] Large amounts of adrenergic neurotransmitters, adrenaline and cortisol, are released increasing heart rate, dilating pupils, slowing digestion and quickening breathing.[15, 32] The hyper-aroused limbic system allows faster reactions for short periods of time to ensure our immediate survival,[25] but compromises effective cognitive functioning through lack of cortical blood flow to the prefrontal cortices, making it difficult to think clearly or problem solve effectively.[32] The brain can also adapt to threatening situations by "freezing", or dissociation from the immediate situation. A person feels emotionally numb, detached from the situation, often curling into the fetal position and adopting neural patterns of avoidance in an effort to protect from further experiences that may be threatening to the basic needs of survival.[25,32]

A child's reaction to trauma and coping skills is dependent on a number of factors:
- Has the child experienced previous trauma?
- Is there a history of psychiatric issues?
- Does he or she have limited coping skills, which may be exacerbated due to the family environment?
- Levels of intelligence and socio-economic status can influence.
- Is there a history of depressive and anxious tendencies?
- Is the family one of dysfunction or relative stability?
- Are there significant 'other' people in the child's life. That is, safe, supportive and caring social supports?
- Did other negative experiences occur after the traumatic indicent?
- Where did the trauma occur? Studies indicate that trauma symptoms are more severe with greater negative reactions if the trauma occurs in a place a child once considered safe.[18,25]

19

Both the events we experience and the qualities nature instilled in us (our genetic predispositions) shape our lives and how we adapt to certain situations.[14]Family environment and caregiver attachments indelibly shape our survival functions and impact our intrinsic memory systems throughout life.[34] Research shows that self-regulation and coping mechanisms are developed through mutual interactions with parents and caregivers from early infancy.[27] Parents may either enhance and amplify a child's up-regulated response to a stressful situation or soothe, calm and support them, thereby down-regulating a child's sympathetic over-arousal stress reaction.

The feeling of safety is essential for children who experience a distressing situation because it down-regulates the hypothalamus-pituitary-adrenal system.[30] When the fear response is triggered, the distress activates the release of the neurochemicals corticotrophin releasing factor (CRF), adrenocorticotrophic hormone, norepinephrine, cortisol and adrenalin. If the fear response is activated frequently, perhaps in situations where the loss a child experiences is not adequately worked through, or the home environment arouses anxiety, the patterns of firing will become established default patterns, easily triggered in future situations of stress and fear.[1]If there is lack of safe interaction between the caregiver and the child, there can develop a trajectory of fear, anxiousness and avoidance behaviours.[10] Instead of a safe environment where there is nurture and the building of resilience and coping skills through difficult circumstances[18] children experiencing scary and traumatic situations can feel overwhelmed or incapacitated.[36] They struggle and need assistance to identify the experienced emotions.[36] It is always within the security of safe attachments that self-regulation and self-soothing capacities can begin to develop.[27]

Safety is fostered when there is empathetic understanding of the loss a child feels. Acknowledging the loss with honest discussions, naming and supporting the child's feelings, identifying with the child the emotional pain associated with loss, working together and supporting changes in the child's life, and assisting the child with effective coping strategies and problem solving skills, can help support the child move forward from the negative effects of a fearful or traumatic situation.[27]

1.5 MEMORY AND STRESS

From the moment of birth our brain is continually processing incoming sensory signals, which begin to form the memories from which we adapt and develop our behaviours.[25] The sensory signals form repetitive patterns as they become familiar and routine during our growth periods, for example, times of feeding, bathing, playing, and so on. Emotions are powerful in memory formation. The pleasure of a mothers touch and gentle care form positive memories in a child. Likewise, experiences that are painful and frightening make a situation highly memorable due to the human brain being primed for protection and survival.

When the activation of such negative emotional memories occurs, an individual may attempt to ensure future avoidance of similar traumatic situations.[21,25] Because fearful memories are encoded in the brain, subsequent reminders of the traumatic event are likely to bring about the same physiological and psychological fear reactions as when the event happened.[6,19,24] If fearful memories are not addressed, the fear response can become generalised and cause the same level of fear whenever there is an inherently innocuous reminder of the traumatic incident, leading to the intrusion of new fears that have no apparent relationship to the original trauma.[6,19] Hypervigilance frequently occurs, and there can be a foreboding sense of impending doom that impinges on a child's ability to engage in normal developmental activities, leading to anxiety driven behaviours and other comorbidities that interfere with healthy adjustment and development.[6]

A child may have difficulty adjusting to a traumatising stressor if:
- They had direct exposure to the traumatic event
- They physically witnessed the trauma
- The event was serious in nature
- The trauma involved the loss of a family member or close loved one.[1]

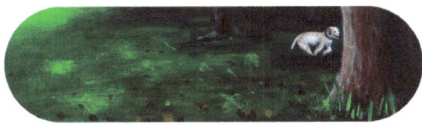

The sometimes prolonged nature of stressful events - as in childhood sexual abuse or domestic violence - where children are regularly and frequently exposed to stressors, results in an over proliferation of glucocorticoids (stress hormones), which can have a negative effect on brain development.[32]   In situations where a child experiences absolute terror, the sympathetic nervous system (the fight or flight instinct) shuts down and we find the child dissociating, moving into a state of unawareness (the freeze response) as the dorsal vagal parasympathetic system is activated.[6,19] Emotional arousal shuts down, heart rate slows and metabolism and blood pressure is lowered in an effort by the brainstem to protect and survive.[30] Situations of intense stress and prolonged stressful events can result in compromised wellness in the limbic area of the brain, hampering neuroplasticity and specifically affecting the hippocampus and the anterior cingulate, adversely affecting memory and learning.[17]

The hippocampus, an important structure in the limbic system is involved in transferring sensory information to the neocortex to consolidate memory. Prolonged exposure to the stress hormones, particulalry glucocorticoids, leads to damage in the hippocampus affecting memory and cognitive function. Brain imaging studies have revealed individuals that have suffered chronic stress, and experience post-traumatic stress disorder (PTSD), may have a less active and smaller hippocampal volume.[30]

Living with a sense of fear and anxiousness results in the instinctive adopting of protection behaviours in order to escape the unpleasant situation. Paranoia and anxiety become common due to the over active and over sensitive amygdala always scanning for potential threats, depressive symptoms are more prevalent,[43] and the child has difficulty managing seemingly low intensity stresses in future situations.[14,30]

This highlights the importance of supporting children who have experienced loss and trauma, providing appropriate, optimal opportunities to move forward, and in so doing, intentionally minimising adverse outcomes.

SECTION 2:

Benson The Boxer: A Psychoeducational Tool For Working With Traumatised Children

2.1 THEORETICAL RATIONALE FOR THE STORY OF BENSON THE BOXER

Statistics reveal that by the age of sixteen, 68 percent of children experience at least one extraordinary event that is frightening and possibly life threatening.[11,12] These are disturbing statistics, and emphasises the need for resources and support to work with traumatised children to build healthy minds and futures, despite the traumatic situations they may experience.[18] Therapists, teachers and parents can assist children to recover from their experience of loss in sensitive, thoughtful and healthy ways.[8] It is however sometimes difficult for adults to connect with children who are grieving and to understand their grief. Often the grief is overlooked or misinterpreted and a career may erroneously conclude that a child's symptoms of loss and grief are simply "difficult attitudes and behaviours."[4]

The *Benson the Boxer* storybook is a psychoeducational tool for working with traumatised children when they have suffered the pain of losing a caring and significant relationship. The primary goal of psychoeducation is to normalise the child's response to the loss and the trauma they have experienced and provide accurate cognitions to the painful and confusing feelings the child may be experiencing.[6]

The purpose of the book *Benson the Boxer* is threefold. First it should be used as a tool to help connect the therapist and the child, second to assist the child in telling their story, and third to encourage the exploration of emotions and feelings.[12] It uses age appropriate language and gives a simple explanation of the human stress response from a neuroscience perspective. The story also gives the therapist the opportunity to provide a safe environment with the use of attentive listening skills, genuine empathy, security and an atmosphere of calm,[37] essential for down-regulating stress and opening new neural pathways.[29,30]

Sharing stories is extremely beneficial for a child because the processes involved in telling and listening engages both the left and right hemispheres of the brain, integrating linguistic processing with emotional, sensorimotor and visual information.[7]

This manual, accompanies the children's story *Benson the Boxer: A Story of Loss and Life*, and focuses on the psychological impact of loss, grief and trauma situations on children. Therefore, it is hoped this tool, for therapists, educators and caregivers, will enhance our understanding of how to talk and work with children who have faced, or who are facing, trauma situations.

Psychoeducation continues throughout therapy with the accompanying Brain Based Worksheets. The worksheets, found at the back of this manual, provide strategies for the individual to manage their current symptoms of fear and anxiety. Finally, the activities in the Brain Based Worksheets are designed to empower and challenge the child and provide them with strategies to cope with future situations of loss and trauma.

2.2 DETAILED OVERVIEW AND EXPLANATION OF BOOK CONTENTS

Cover/Introduction

The inside cover invites any child who has experienced loss, or has been in a frightening situation, to read the book. Age is not specified here, due to appropriate age being subjective and dependent on so many variables and circumstances.

The Story

The story begins as a normal day in the life of *Benson the Boxer dog*, but turns into one of intense trauma when he witnesses his best friend Lucy Labrador killed by a truck.

The book takes the reader and listener on a journey of traumatic experience, grief, physiological pain, as well as unfounded guilt. It identifies feelings of fear, numbness, confusion and sadness as normal emotions associated with trauma and grief.[18]

Throughout the story there is opportunity for children to engage with the life of Benson and his friends. It allows and encourages the exploration of Bensons character:

- What sort of dog was he? What character traits?
- There can be discussion regarding his special friendship with Lucy.
- Exploration into the lives of the other animals in the story.
- Talk about friendships and special people in our lives, those we connect with.
- What is the relationship of the other animals to Benson?
- There can be an imaginative discussion into the strange and friendly farmyard animals. Why might Benson think they were strange?
- Discussion can also centre around the special characteristics of Uncle Boris and why Benson knew he could trust him. This can lead into exploration of the special people the child trusts, those he or she feels safe with, and who they feel they can talk to.

There are many other possible themes that can be discussed in relation to the story of Benson the Boxer. Some examples include:

- The care and concern for Benson by the other animals.
- The remembrance dinner held in honour of Lucy, a way of celebrating a life.
- Setting up of rituals to remember loved ones.
- Normative grieving behaviours: fatigue, restlessness, weakness, sadness, emotional distancing from people, irritable and maybe angry, purposeless activity.[43]
- Building a sense of safety with others that we trust, just as Benson did with Uncle Boris.

Every painted picture in the book tells the story, as the artist has deliberately added features of interest to every page. Taking time to interact with each picture, noticing the details, discussing what can be seen and imagining what cannot be seen, can further add to the enjoyment of the book and enhance the feeling of safety, whereby children are more willing to engage in positive approach goals.

Reflection opportunities

There are natural "breaks" in the story, identifiable by a noticeable repeat of the picture of a very miserable Benson and the words "*Benson the Boxer feels miserable*", or a similar expression, where the therapist, teacher or parent can:

- Stop and discuss individual emotions
- Pause and use silence to let the story be absorbed
- Provide time for the child to express his or her personal thoughts
- Provide opportunity to just sit and "hold the space" of grief.
- Provide time and "permission" for the child to reflect and grieve.

Moving beyond the story

The *Benson the Boxer* story ends with Benson recognising he would like to get well and suggesting to Uncle Boris that he would like to go outside again, rather than being stuck inside, trapped by his fears. Benson discovers he can move forward, even though he will never forget his friend and companion.

This ending is not intended to indicate that therapy stops when an individual recognises his or her need for help, or when a client states they would like to make changes. For children who have experienced a traumatic loss, the trauma symptoms may have interfered with the child's ability to experience a typical grieving process. Therefore, once the trauma symptoms have abated, the child is then able to begin the grieving process with the support of the therapist.[6]

The final pages of the book show specific pictures of a young boy and a young girl in a position of physical and emotional withdrawal. Children who experience loss and trauma experience a profound change in the way they see the world, other people and themselves.[6] These final pictures can be used to encourage the child to share their own personal story as they identify with the expression and the posture and the children in the paintings.

Appropriate questions to invite discussion could include:

- What do you think has happened to this child?
- What do you think he or she is thinking?
- What do think he or she is feeling?
- Have you ever sat like this? When?
- What comes into your head when you look at these pictures?
- Where are the other members of his or her family (mother, father, sisters, brothers and others)?
- What do you think has happened?
- Why is he or she feeling upset?
- What would you like to tell her or him?
- Does this picture remind you of someone you know?
- If this were you in the picture, what would you be thinking?
- If this were you, who would you like to come and sit with you?

Naming emotions

It is recommended that picture cards be used to explore a child's feelings, rather than the words alone. Many websites are available to purchase or download resources for use in therapy. Common websites can be accessed by searching for "feelings charts" or "emotions charts".

2.3 THEMES THROUGHOUT THE BOOK

The Therapeutic Alliance

The therapeutic alliance is recognised as the strongest predictor of positive and effective counselling outcomes.[37] This is no less true when counselling children and teenagers as concluded by Geldard, Geldard and Foo (2013) who confirm a positive therapeutic alliance is the single most important factor in achieving successful therapeutic outcomes with young people.

There is a clear demonstration of appropriate attending skills used by the story character Uncle Boris (the therapist), and a therapeutic alliance based on a bottom-up approach of safety, client control, and empathetic understanding.[30] The dialogue in the book depicts genuine care, calming vocal qualities, gentle speech, attentive listening skills, as well as the appropriate use of silence,[16] which can offer guidance and enhance skills for any therapist.

Safety

The importance of the therapeutic alliance aligns with the critical role of the client experiencing safety in order to establish new and more effective patterns of neural firing.[1] Thinking patterns and decision-making is compromised when an individual experiences a traumatic situation, leading to the adoption of unhelpful behavioural patterns.[31] The nervous system processes the traumatic situation from a sensory "bottom up" aspect; therefore, as the client reprocesses the trauma they may feel distress and a lack of control. Only when there is a perception of safety, facilitated by a secure and empathetic therapist, can new strategies be attempted and change can be facilitated.[1,32]

A safe environment down-regulates stress, leading to higher intellectual analysis of a situation, enhancing the perception of control, thereby placing the client in a situation in which the therapist can address unhelpful patterns of neural activation and enable more functional outcomes.[32]

The neuroscience underpinning fear, anxious thoughts and behaviours

Neuroscience concepts can be difficult to explain to young children due to the complexity of the terminology and the biology, which are mostly beyond a child's understanding. Siegel and Payne Bryson (2012) report, however, that even small children can understand some basics of how the brain works, which provides important understanding of their personal feelings and behaviours, along with normalising their emotions.[23] The storybook, *Benson the Boxer*, outlines, in simple language, a basic neurobiological explanation of the physiological and psychological results of the stress response and our memory systems following a traumatic event.

Patterns of approach

The therapist's goal is to promote patterns of approach, whereby the child feels safe and confident to attempt new behaviours. Patterns of approach develop when the basic human needs, outlined by Grawe (2007) are fulfilled.[14] The basic needs include: the need for control, the need for attachment, the need for distress avoidance and pleasure maximisation, and the need for self-esteem protection and self enhancement.[14,32]

Avoidance behaviours

In a situation of loss and trauma, whether on-going trauma, or a highly traumatic experience, it is common for the individual to adopt avoidance behaviours. This is due to the traumatic experience heightening the natural fear response designed to keep us safe from a perceived threat. It is when this adaptive and necessary fear mechanism becomes exagerated and over stimulated that it moves beyond keeping us safe, becomes maladaptive and we feel paralysed by fear.[14] In an attempt to protect from further physical, social or emotional pain the individual adopts protective avoidance behaviours.[32,30] The brain essentially re-organises itself to survive. This is achieved through modification of an individual's behavioural response to their environment. A sense of potential threats, alerts and unease is aroused, resulting in behaviours of withdrawal and isolation in order to feel safe.[25,30 32] Depressive tendencies and dissociations commonly surface and an individual is robbed of a normal healthy life.[32]

The story of *Benson the Boxer* highlights avoidance behaviours commonly used in order to protect. It brings awareness that these same avoidance behaviours can also inhibit the individual from engaging in the activities they once enjoyed and outlines how an individual can become stuck in behaviour patterns that promote unwellness.[2]

Guilt

The reality and the abruptness of trauma is often confusing for children, and many experience feelings of guilt, shame, social isolation and fearfulness concerning the future.[22] Children under the age of six are cognitively immature with a narrowly focused attention, which often leads to confusion and an inability to understand cognitive perspectives, so they may mistakenly think the event is their fault.[18] This book can be used as a platform to discuss the emotions of guilt and shame commonly associated with situations of loss.

Strengths and protective factors

The end of the book outlines the strengths and protective factors of the character Benson, with the last pages suggesting Benson is at the beginning of the road to recovery. The identified protective factors include the support of friends and prior displays of strength and courage when in crisis situations. The last page of the book has the therapist (Uncle Boris) offering ongoing care and encouragement with the statement of, *"I'll come with you"*. This is intended to indicate to the child that they are not alone, but can continue to rely on the therapist, the teacher or the parent, and others, for support as they begin their journey to wellness.

Acknowledging the individual child

This book respects and values individual emotional feelings and behaviours, and avoids the automatic response of intrusively attempting to "fix" the child's problems.[35] It does not overtly acknowledge all treatment approaches, but joins with the child and gives opportunity to work out solutions together, leaving the reader (child) and the therapist open to treatments appropriate to the individual, recognising that every situation is unique.[42]

Change and growth

The book assists the development of problem solving and decision-making skills, recognising that children, despite their age and naiveté, are also required to make choices, take risks and explore options.[12] There is opportunity to acknowledge possible changes and growth, and then engage in a discussion about how the traumatic experiences may have strengthened the individual. The child could be encouraged to construct a future positive ending for Benson, which ideally could lead to incorporating these "future positive" ideas to his/her own life.

Sleep disorders and general health

The story outlines sleep disorders which may be experienced as a result of stressful situations and provides the opportunity to explain to the child the work of the hippocampus in memory development, and the necessity of good rest and quality sleep. Additionally, the child can be introduced to calming activities such as mindfulness, meditation, regulated breathing and relaxation techniques.

An important fuel source, brain-derived neurotrophic factor (BDNF) is essential in counteracting the effects of cortisol which accompanies psychosocial stress.[41] Increasing Omega-3's into the diet, limiting sugar intake, cognitive stimulation, regular quality sleep and engaging in exercise enhances the production of brain-derived neurotrophic factor (BDNF), which acts on the nervous system to engage adaptive responses to changing environmental demands.[4]

Choice and client control

Providing the child with choice, promotes a sense of control and orientation.[14] Control is about manipulating or regulating the environment or our relationships to satisfy and achieve personal goals. We feel a sense of control when we have options and when there is understanding or an accurate appraisal of a situation.[14] At a time when the child feels vulnerable, scared, guilty, perplexed and helpless,[11] providing situations where there is an element of control will begin to restore psychological congruence.[14]

Simple choices for the child may include:
- Who will hold the book while reading?
- Who will turn the pages?
- Would they like to hold a puppet or a soft toy while reading the story?
- Where would they like to sit?
- Which pictures did they enjoy the most?
- Is there a section of the story they would like to read again?

2.4 RECOMMENDED AGE GROUPS AND ACCOMPANYING WORKSHEETS

Recognising that children often find it difficult to express their emotions, because they can be hidden from conscious awareness,[12] the book *Benson the Boxer* is written predominantly, though not exclusively, for children between the ages of 4 to 12+ years old. It could be argued that children are literal thinkers so may not identify the story of the boxer dog with their own situation, but studies have shown that children, by the age of four years old, are able to distinguish literal from nonliteral truths.[39] We would expect therefore that many children within this age range will be able to identify with Benson's traumatic experience and relate it to a similar experience of their own, and in-so-doing gain greater insight into their own responses.

The *Benson the Boxer* storybook is accompanied by a Junior and Senior Brain Based Activity Worksheets, both found within this manual. The worksheet activities compliment the Benson story, highlighting the neuroscience behind fear and anxiety as a result of the loss and trauma Benson experienced. The story of *Benson the Boxer* specifically looks at the concept of grief and loss, however, the worksheets can be applied to any situation where a child experiences traumatic changes in their life; for example, parental separation and divorce, moving interstate, changing schools, experiencing a natural disaster, living in a country where there is political unrest and war related traumas, chronic illness or an injury that leaves a child with a disability.

The worksheets are designed to be simple, by not simplistic in their approach to neuroscience. Unlike a classroom situation where workbook content is curriculum focused and driven by the need for a student to progress to the next level or benchmark, these worksheets are designed to open discussion, provide enjoyment, foster a positive therapeutic alliance and provide a platform to build a child's knowledge and understanding of avoidant behaviours developed when experiencing fear and anxiety. The worksheets lead a child through situations of controllable incongruence that can help transform existing neural networks and move a child towards behavioural patterns of approach.

Both the Junior and Senior Brain Based Worksheet activities are colourful, user-friendly and provide enjoyable activities. The activities in both the Junior and Senior books are similar in content, but the language is adapted and modified to suit the specified age groups. The Senior Worksheets provide more detailed activities, however it would not be unusual for a child to work between the two workbooks, as each activity is a beneficial tool for the therapist, teacher or parent to expand on, ask questions about or evaluate a child's thoughts and feelings, and can be adapted to the needs of the individual child and the different therapy situations that arise.

The Junior Brain Based Activity Worksheets:

These are recommended for children between 4-7 years old. This is a time when internal language is developing along with the development of verbal and visual memory.[38] Cause and effect become recognizable by the age of 5 years old and children in this age bracket enjoy stories and love being read to.[38] Between the ages of 4-7 children enjoy copying letters and doing designs and drawings, therefore the Brain Based Activity Worksheets provide many activities to encourage self-expression through art and colouring. The activities promote emotional awareness and give a basic understanding of memory and memory formation. As a child completes the worksheet activities they will discover strategies to move forward to a place of wellness.

The Senior Brain Based Activity Worksheets:

These are recommended for children between the ages of 8-12+. The activities are colourful, enjoyable and appealing to the developing mind of a pre-teen. They are not designed to be difficult in content, but rather provide opportunity to expand on the many and varied emotions relating to the young person's experience of loss. Sprenger (2008) outlines that eight to twelve year olds are able to articulate their feelings and are often highly sensitive. They like drama and adventure and are usually curious about life and growing up. This age group wants explanations and reasons, thrives on choice and loves competition.

This is an age where children can identify their own feelings. Therefore, throughout the workbook children are encouraged to name their own personal feelings and identify the situations and perceived emotional experiences of others.

The worksheet activities are varied and allow for creative expression in the drawings, activities and colouring-in pages, however, the Brain Based Activity Worksheets offer more than just fun activities that a child completes after reading the storybook *Benson the Boxer*. The purpose of both the Junior and Senior worksheets is to enable a child to engage in activities that enhance patterns of approach rather than adopting, or continuing, patterns of avoidance.

Patterns of approach and new learning occurs when the child feels safe and experiences their situation to be within their window of tolerance (controlled incongruence).[32] In a situation of loss, fear and anxiety increases as the individual tries to make sense of the tragic situation. When anxiety increases the left Pre Frontal Cortex is unable to modulate emotional arousal in the right Pre Frontal Cortex and the limbic system. This results in over-reactive behavioural responses and feelings of uncontrollable incongruence.[14] It is therefore a normative reaction to want to withdraw when experiencing a situation of loss as the uncontrollable incongruence increases the individual's neurophysiological fear arousal, resulting in protective behaviours of avoidance and withdrawal in an attempt to stop the emotional pain.[14]

It is the goal of the worksheet activities to increase connectivity and modulate control over the amygdala's overreactions. Providing a safe environment of enjoyment and engagment activates the Right Pre Frontal Cortex, opening neural pathways and increasing blood flow to the cortical brain regions where new learning takes place.[29]   Right-brain to right-brain interaction between the adult and the child down-regulates the stress response, provides safe opportunities to share emotional fears and ultimately has a positive effect on developing strategies for mastering stress responses in the future.[29]

It is important to note that these Brain Based Activity Worksheets are designed as a tool to aid the therapeutic process. Therefore, it is highly recommended that a child enjoy the activities in conjunction with, and guided by, a therapist, teacher, parent or carer. Children will enjoy completing the activities independently, but there should be no expectation that a child will complete the activities alone. In fact, it is recommended that the activities are enjoyed together with a present and caring adult, thereby strengthening a therapeutic and supportive relationship and providing opportunities for questions, discussion, empathetic engagement and therapy work.

2.5 GUIDELINES FOR EDUCATORS AND PARENTS

When loss is experienced, children may quickly become attached to others outside their family.[4] Many children view their teacher as a "secure" attachment figure due to the caring and nurture they receive on a daily basis. Children also find involving a trusted person away from the immediate family environment can provide opportunity to share their grief, without being continually overwhelmed by a home situation that may be heavy with sadness of the loss. A teacher is often able to facilitate more open communication with a grieving student,[4] therefore having a basic understanding of the way a child may respond to loss, along with the neuroscience of grief, fear, loss and trauma is imperative in order to promote healthy recovery.

Benson the Boxer can be successfully used in individual counselling sessions, in small groups, or in larger classroom environments. The story and Brain Based Activity Worksheets are designed to bring emotional awareness to students and help them identify normal fear reactions when experiencing situations that are bad, sad or scary. Written from a neuroscience perspective it will explain to students the physiological changes that occur when they become frightened, and why they behave or respond in the way they do. It outlines the importance of talking with someone whom they trust, and provides strategies on how to move from a state of being trapped in a state of psychological un-wellness to surviving and thriving.

It is imperative that the teacher has established a safe and empathetic classroom environment where there is trust and respect, not only for the teacher, but also between student peers.[7] Children who have experienced a significant loss and/or trauma can react unpredictably and negatively when they feel uncomfortable or emotionally unsafe.[4,15] If a child becomes fearful or anxious, they will activate and rely on the lower and faster regions of the brain (survival brain) rather than the thinking cortical brain regions, and out of fear, anger, embarrassment or frustration they may erupt into a behavioural tirade or withdraw and refuse to participate.[15]

These behaviours can become particularly apparent if the child's loss is due to parental death, separation or abandonment.[4] It is therefore advisable for a teacher to guide the worksheet activities with their students, rather than have the children attempt this workbook as an independent learning activity.

If a teacher observes discomfort or negative reactions while using the worksheets, it is advisable that a school counsellor or therapist is available to talk with individual students about how they feel and guide them into feeling safe. This needs to be done discreetly, without embarrassing or singling out students who may express difficult or problematic emotional reactions.

2.6 INTEGRATING THEORETICAL APPROACHES

The story of *Benson the Boxer* incorporates Freud's psychodynamic therapies of "consciousness raising",[26] but also introduces cognitive behaviour therapies which challenge and confront irrational beliefs such as unfounded guilt and negative self-talk.[5] Empathy, unconditional positive regard, authenticity and congruence, active listening and non-directive techniques, advocated by Carl Rogers,[12] are a predominant focus of the story book. Through such approaches a therapist may promote awareness of emotional feelings and current experiences so that change for the client can take place and assist in what Gestalt theorists describe as an "Ah-ha" experience, a defining moment of feeling integrated and an ability to move forward.[12]

The story provides an excellent platform when using narrative therapy, because it not only encourages a child to share in personal story telling, but may also be used to assist a child to create an alternative story for their own narrative, by formulating a new and preferred story.[12] A combination of puppets, soft toys and a story dialogue helps a child to make personal connections, enabling the linking of characters in the story with their own feelings and personal narrative.[12]

Neuropsychotherapy is the over-arching "umbrella" modality that outlines trauma and loss from a neuroscience perspective, providing a framework for understanding that the physiological and psychological effects activate the stress response in order to protect the individual and provide consistency.[14,32] It incorporates a brain-based approach of providing an environment of safety, which can gradually shift the patterns of avoidance a child has adopted in order to protect him or herself, and move the child forward to patterns of approach.[1]

2.7 ADDITIONAL IDEAS FOR THERAPISTS

The following ideas contribute to effective brain-based therapies in that they provide experiences for the child which are engaging and are perceived as play.[12] Because most children are not voluntary clients, there may be anxiousness surrounding the new environment in which therapy is provided,[20] therefore using play to compliment the story of *Benson the Boxer*, would down-regulate emotional fears.

Providing a multitude of sensory stimulation opportunities at one time could be overwhelming to the child,[20] but suggesting the child can choose a medium, each session, provides opportunities to experience a sense of control, especially if there are a number of options available.[14]

Clay: The use of clay where the child could sculpt and mould various emotional expressions relating to the story (for example; sadness, guilt, fear, anger).[12]

Artwork: Drawing or colouring the story ending - a '"what happens" scenario to foster discussion of how to help Benson become well, which would enable the therapist to discuss how trauma has affected the child and provide options for promoting wellness.[12]

Sand play: A sand tray with the use of miniature animals (plastic dogs) for exploring the past, the trauma situation itself and any associated fears.[12] Fantasy is often used in order to provide light relief and provides an avenue for expressing personal emotions.[9] It also assists the therapist to determine the emotional maturity and cognitive ability of the child.[12]

Soft toys and Puppets: Puppets and soft toys add an extra dimension to storytelling, allowing the child to become directly involved through manipulation of the puppets and in dialogue with the story.[12]

Pictures: The pictures in the storybook can be used in isolation from the story, as they portray a number of emotions that a child would identify with and assist the child in expressing how they feel, without the struggle of finding the right words.[20]

Internal movie player: When a child finds it too painful to retell a traumatic experience they can be introduced to the internal movie player, which allows the child to replay the experience in his or her mind but uses an imaginary remote to stop, pause, fast forward and rewind the story when they need to.[36] The therapist could use the story of *Benson the Boxer* to illustrate how to do this, later encourage the child to share their story using the technique. The internal movie player provides an element of control and helps in the organisation and the orientation of the events, which assists in integrating implicit and explicit memories.[36]

Mazes: There are a number of mazes within the worksheet activities which have been designed to portray life situations as a journey. The Brain Maze (P154) in the Senior Workbook can be used as is a whole learning activity for both younger children and teenagers. The Brain Maze starts in the brain stem and moves through the cerebellum and the occipital lobe where the child "travels" along alleyways such as Panic Path, Stress Street, Anxious Ally, Lonely Lane (the Survival Brain). The journey takes them past the amygdala (Amy G'Dala) who is warning them to withdraw, run and hide. Moving past the amygdala into the cortical brain areas, the path takes them around Choice Corner, Courage Court, Bravery Boulevard and so on, until they exit beside Benson. The maze provides opportunity for specific areas of the brain to be explored, particularly the reactive limbic system that initiates the "fight or flight" response. It acknowledges common emotional responses, with the lanes and alleyways being specifically named to give understanding of the amygdala's immediate fear reaction before it consults the executive brain where reasoning, rational thinking and problem solving occur. It also highlights that moving forward, towards wellness, begins with courage, bravery, determination and choice.

Caution:

If a child does not wish to engage with the book, the therapist is advised to put the book aside, avoiding any expression of personal disappointment, but rather explore what is behind the child's rejection of the story and emotional state.[12]

There could be a number of reasons that must be respected:

- The child may feel uncomfortable, emotionally or physically
- They may have a fear of dogs
- There may be a negative association with reading or story telling
- There could be underlying issues hidden in their unconsciousness that have been triggered

If the child's choice is not respected, fear responses will be activated raising defenses and likely resulting in an immediate shut-down of logical thinking and effective communication.[35]

2.8 HELPING A CHILD REGAIN CONTROL[40]

3-R's

Reassure the child that what is happening to them is normal.

Remind the child that these feelings start to get better once their brain system settles down. Slow, controlled breathing techniques help calm a heightened "survival brain".

Restore their trust by offering genuine empathy, understanding, care and a safe environment.

General Ideas to help a child after loss

- Encourage the continuation of activities: School attendance, sporting activities and social events.

- Stay connected: Encourage frequent talking and sharing with someone the child trusts.

- Honest discussions: Answer questions gently but honestly. Hiding information can lead to distrust.

- Keep them informed: Telling a child what to expect, changes they may encounter, what events/memorials/family gatherings are happening gives opportunity to emotionally prepare and provides a sense of control.

- Express emotions: If talking is difficult encourage journaling, drawing, painting, sculpting, building or creating.

- Allow for ceremonies and rituals: Light a candle, plant a tree, collect keepsakes, make a memory scrapbook.

- Stay active. Set goals to do something active, playful and fun everyday.

- Eat well: Nutritious food promotes both physical and mental health.

- Sleep hygiene: Regular bed times. Reading before sleep, a soft light, relaxing music, soothing massage encourages tiredness.

- Quiet times: Give opportunity for relaxation, mindfulness and breathing activities during the day - away from technology, social media and distractions.

- Let a child grieve in their own way - there is no time frame or "right" way to grieve.

REFERENCES

1. Allison, K. & Rossouw, P. J. (2013). The therapeutic alliance: Exploring the concept of "safety" from a neuropsychotherapeutic perspective. International Journal of Neuropsychotherapy. 1, pp 21-29 doi: 10.12744/ijnpt.2013.0021-0029

2. Arden, J. B. & Linford, L. (2009). Brain-based therapy and the 'Pax Medica'. Psychotherapy in Australia, 15(3), pp16-23.

3. Bonanno, G. (2004). Loss, trauma, and human resilience: Have we underestimated the human capacity to thrive after extremely aversive events? The American Psychologist, 59(1), pp 20-28.

4. Burns, D.M. (2010). When kids are grieving: Addressing grief and loss in school. Thousand Oaks, CA: Corwin Press.

5. Clark, L. (2002). SOS help for emotions: Managing anxiety, anger and depression (2nd ed.). Bowling Green USA: SOS Programs & Parents Press. Retrieved from www.sosprograms.com

6. Cohen, J. A., Mannarino, A. P., & Deblinger, E. (2006). Treating trauma and traumatic grief in children and adolescents: A clinician's guide. Retrieved from http://wwweblib.com.

7. Cozolino, L. (2013). The social neuroscience of education: Optimizing attachment & learning in the classroom. New York: W.W. Norton & Co.

8. Cronin Favazza, P., & Munson, L.J. (2010). Loss And Grief In Young Children. Young Exceptional Children, 13(2), pp 86-99.

9. Ennis, J. (1999, September). Creative and practical counselling and psychotherapy for child and adult trauma victims. Presentation, Restoration for Victims of Crime Conference Australian Institute of Criminology and Victims Referral and Assistance Service, Melbourne. Retrieved from http://www.aic.gov.au/media_library/conferences/rvc/ennis.pdf

10. Eppel, A. (2013). Attachment and Loss: Matters of life and death. New Therapist: Indispensable Survival Guide for the Thinking Psychotherapist, 84, The Neuro Edition (Part 2), unpaginated. Retrieved from http://eppelreport.blogspot.com.au/2013/03/attachment-and-loss-matters-of-life-and.html (accessed, September 2016).

11. Everstine, D. S., & Everstine, L. (2013). Strategic interventions for people in crisis, trauma, and disaster: (Revised 2nd ed). Hoboken: Taylor and Francis.

12. Geldard, K., Geldard, D., & Foo, R. Y. (2013). Counselling children (4th ed.). London: SAGE.

13. Goldman, L. (2000). Life and loss: A guide to helping grieving children (2nd ed.). Philadelphia: Accelerated Development.

14. Grawe, K. (2007). Neuropsychotherapy: How the neurosciences inform effective psychotherapy. Mahwah, N.J: Lawrence Erlbaum.

15. Howard, J. A. (2013). Distressed or Deliberately Defiant: Managing challenging student behaviour due to trauma and disorganised attachment. Toowong, Qld: Australian Academic Press.

16. Ivy, A. E. (2010). Intentional interviewing and counselling: Facilitating client development in a multicultural society (7th ed.). Belmont, CA: Brooks/Cole.

17. Jensen, F.E., (2015). The teenage brain: A neuroscientist's survival guide to raising adolescents and young adults. New York, NY: Harper Collins.

18. Joshi, P., Lewin, S., & O'Donnell, D. (2005). The handbook of frequently asked questions following traumatic events: Violence, disasters, or terrorism. Washington, D.C: International Center To Heal Our Children: Building Healthy Minds and Futures. Retrieved from http://childrensnational.org/~/media/cnhs-site/files/resources/ichoc/handbook.ashx?la=en

19. Linden, M. & Rutkowski, K (Eds.)(2013). Hurting memories and beneficial forgetting: Posttraumatic stress disorders, biographical developments, and social conflicts. Amsterdam, Netherlands: Elsevier Inc.

20. Lukas, S. R. (1993). Where to start and what to ask: An assessment handbook (1st ed.). New York: W.W. Norton & Co.

21. Medina, J. (2014). Brain rules: 12 principles for surviving and thriving at work, home, and school. Seattle: Pear Press.

22. Maxmen, J. S., Ward, N. G., & Kilgus, M. D. (2009). Essential psychopathology and its treatment (3rd ed.). New York: W.W. Norton & Co.

23. Neuner, F., Schauer, M., Klaschik, C., Karunakara, U., & Elbert, T. (2004). A comparison of narrative exposure therapy, supportive counseling, and psychoeducation for treating posttraumatic stress disorder in an African refugee settlement. Journal of Consulting and Clinical, 72 (4), pp 579-87.

24. Noel, M., Chambers, C. T., Mcgrath, P. J., Klein, R. M., Stewart. S. H. (2012). The influence of children's pain memories on subsequent pain experience. August, 2012, Vol.153(8), p.1563(10).

25. Perry, B. D., & Szalavitz, M. (2006). The boy who was raised as a dog and other stories from a child psychiatrist's notebook: What traumatized children can teach us about loss, love, and healing. New York: Basic Books.

26. Prochaska, J. O., & Norcross, J. C. (2010). Systems of psychotherapy: A transtheoretical analysis. Belmont, CA: Cengage Learning.

27. Ringel, S. (2012). Attachment theory, infant research, and neurobiology. In S. Ringel & J. Brandell (Eds.), Trauma: Contemporary directions in theory, practice, and research (pp 77-96). Thousand Oaks, CA: SAGE Publications Ltd. doi: 10.4135/9781452230597.n5

28. Roberts, M. (2011). Grief, loss and trauma: Frequent visitors to school communities. Grief Matters: The Australian Journal Of Grief And Bereavement, (14), 1, pp 8-10.

29. Rossouw, P. J. (2012a). Engaging in therapy and history taking: Right brain to right brain communication. Neuropsychotherapy in Australia, 17, pp 3-8. Retrieved from http://mediros.com.au/wp-content/uploads/2012/11/NPTIG-e-journal-17.pdf (accessed September 2016).

30. Rossouw, P. J. (2012b). Neurobiological markers of childhood trauma: Implications for therapeutic interventions. Neuropsychotherapy in Australia, 16, pp. 3-8. Retrieved from http://mediros.com.au/wp-content/uploads/2012/11/NPTIG-e-journal-16.pdf (accessed September 2016).

31. Rossouw, P. J. (2013). The end of the medical model? Recent findings in neuroscience regarding antidepressant medication: Implications for neuropsychotherapy. Neuropsychotherapy in Australia, 19, pp. 3-10. Retrieved from http://www.mediros.com.au/wp-content/uploads/2013/01/Neuropsychotherapy-in-Australia-E-Journal-Edition-19.pdf (accessed, September 2016).

32. Rossouw, P. J. (Ed.) (2014). Neuropsychotherapy: Theoretical underpinnings and clinical applications. Brisbane, QLD: Mediros Pty Ltd.

33. Rynearson, E. K. (Ed.). (2006). Violent death: Resilience and intervention beyond the crisis. New York: Routledge.

34. Schore, J. R., & Schore, A. N. (2007). Modern attachment theory: The central role of affect regulation in development and treatment. Clinical Social Work Journal, 36, (1), pp 9–20. doi:10.1007/s10615-007-0111-7

35. Siegel, D., & Hartzell, M. (2004). Parenting from the inside out: How a deeper self-understanding can help you raise children who thrive (1st ed.). New York: J.P. Tarcher/Penguin.

36. Siegel, D., & Payne Bryson, T. (2012). The whole-brain child: 12 revolutionary strategies to nurture your child's developing mind. New York: Scribe Publications.

37. Sommers-Flanagan, R., & Sommers-Flanagan, J. (2009). Clinical interviewing (4th ed.). New Jersey: John Wiley & Sons.

38. Sprenger, M. (2008). The developing brain: Birth to age eight. Thousand Oaks, CA: Sage Publications.

39. Vosniadou, S. (1987). Children and Metaphors. Child Development, 58(3), pp 870–885. http://doi.org/10.2307/1130223

40. White, J. (2006). Coping with trauma: A talking therapies service for people across Thurrock. South East Glasgow: South East Glasgow Community Health & Care Partnership. Retrieved from http://inclusionthurrock.org/wp-content/uploads/2016/03/IT-Booklet-Coping-with-trauma-V1.pdf (accessed September 2106).

41. Wilson, R. Z. (2014). Neuroscience for counsellors: Practical applications for counsellors, therapists and mental health practitioners.London and Philadelphia: Jessica Kingsley Publishers.

42. Yalom, I. D. (2009). The gift of therapy : An open letter to a new generation of therapists and their patients (1st Harper Perennial ed.). New York : Harper Perennial.

43. Zisook, S., & Devaul, R. A. (1983). Grief, unresolved grief, and depression. Psychosomatics, 24 (3), pp 247-56.

JUNIOR
WORKBOOK

For ages 4-7

CONTENTS

Hi there!

Hi there kids,

Welcome to Benson the Boxer Worksheets.

These worksheets are so cool! The activities will help explain why you feel the way you do when something bad, sad or scary happens. They will also give ideas on how to feel better if you ever feel scared or sad again.

If you feel yukky or sad when doing the worksheets, just pause and talk to someone you trust.

I am so glad we are going to have more time together.

Let's go,

Benson

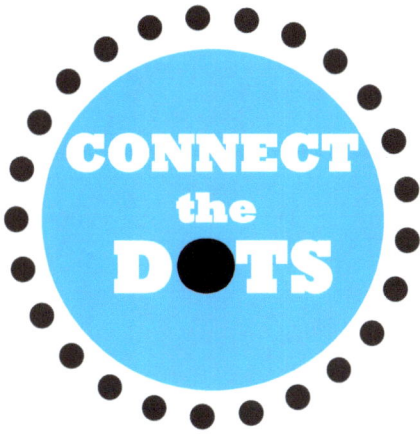

CONNECT the DOTS

1 •• 82

2 •
     • 81

3 •
     • 80

4 •   • 79
       • 78 77   76 •   74 •
5 •   •   75 •
6 •

7 •

8 •

9 •   31 • 32 •   35 •
               33 • 34 •
10 •
11 •   • 30
                             36 •

           • 21   37 •

12 •   • 29
      22 • • 28
    20 •   • 27
13 •   23 •   • 26   38 •
            24 • 25 •
       19 •   39 •
14 •   • 18
15 •   • 17   40 •
    16 •
                         41 •
                 42 •   43 •

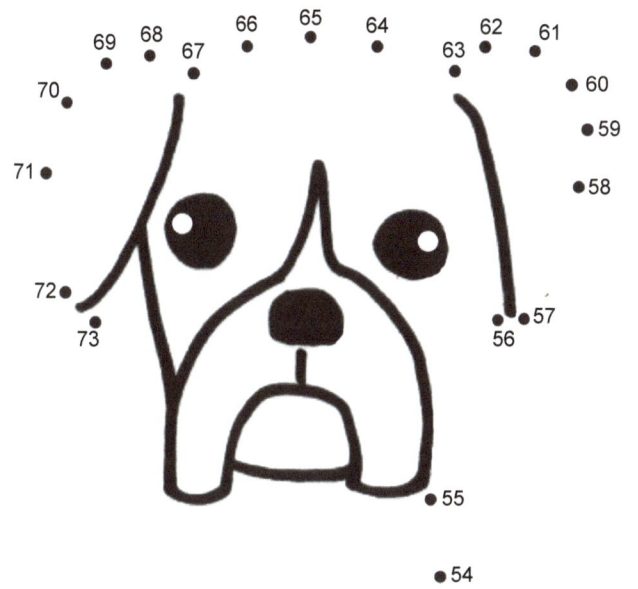

69 • 68 •   66 •   65 •   64 •   62 •   61 •
70 •   67 •   63 •   • 60
                              • 59
71 •   • 58
72 •   57 •
   73 •   56 •

                     • 55

                   • 54

                     • 53

                     • 52

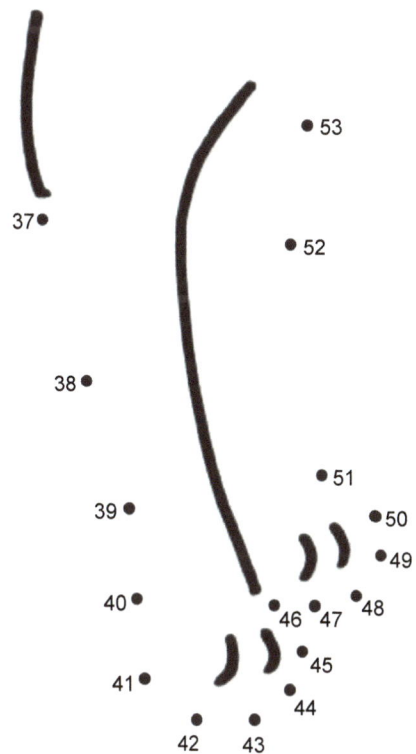

                  • 51
                   • 50
                     • 49
                   • 48
46 • 47 •
             • 45
            44 •

60

Put the following pictures in order of when they happened

1. Benson and Lucy playing
2. The ball rolling onto the road
3. Benson hiding and staying inside
4. Benson with Uncle Boris talking and going outside again

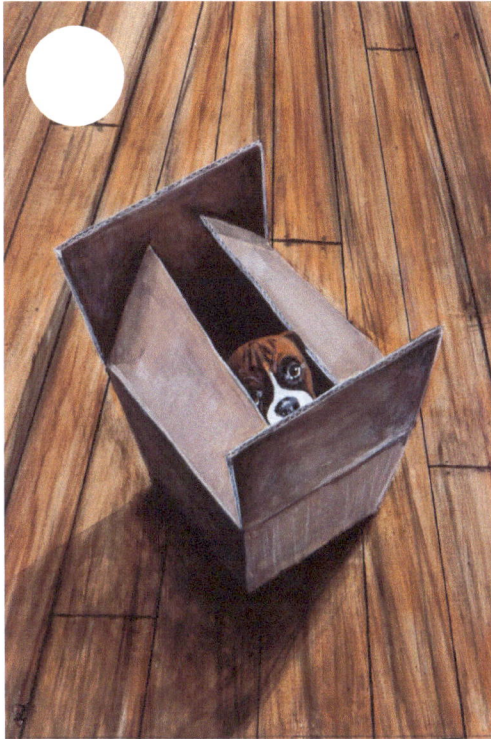

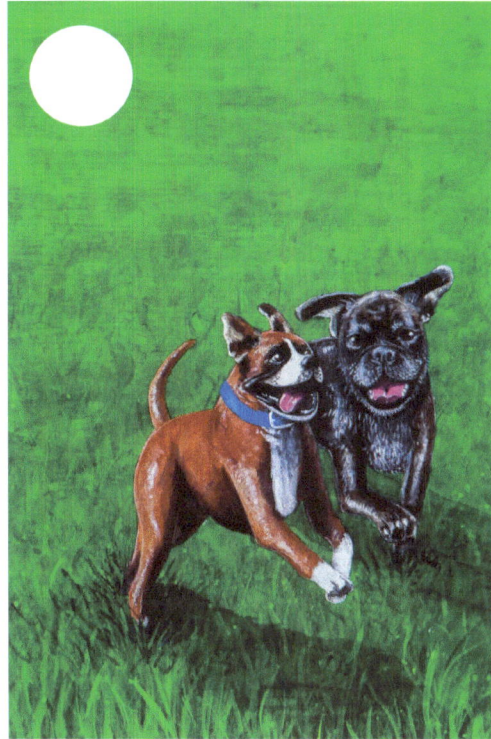

I'm famous!

COLOUR BENSON IN BY NUMBERS

1 = BLUE   2 = BROWN   3 = GREEN   4 = WHITE   5 = BLACK

Look at each picture and colour in the
circle next to the correct answer.

- ○ Benson is playing
- ○ Benson is hiding
- ○ Benson is frightened
- ○ Benson is sad

- ○ Benson is happy
- ○ Benson is excited
- ○ Benson is miserable
- ○ Benson is sleeping

- ○ Benson is weak and afraid
- ○ Benson is hiding
- ○ Benson is brave, strong
- ○ Benson is sitting

- ○ Benson is remembering
- ○ Benson is laughing
- ○ Benson is playing
- ○ Benson is walking

66

Draw a picture of something **FUN**
Benson and Lucy loved to do together.

4 FEELINGS

Colour, cut out and match the picture to each feeling

HAPPY	**SAD**
SCARED	**ANGRY**

Draw an experience that could make someone feel really **HAPPY!**

Draw an experience that could make someone feel really SAD!

Draw an experience that could make someone feel really SCARED!

Draw an experience that could make someone feel really ANGRY!

MEMORY MAKING

Our brain is like a super smart movie maker. It records things we see, things we feel, things we hear, things we taste and things we smell.

Sight, touch, hearing, taste and smell are called our senses.

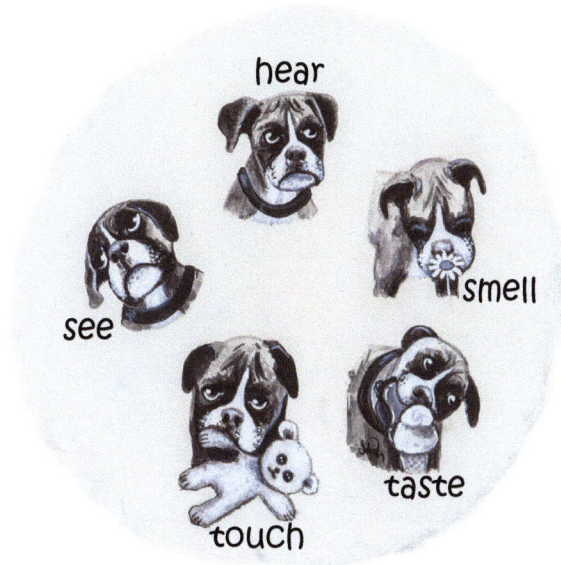

hear

see

smell

touch

taste

Things we see, things we feel, things we hear, things we taste and things we smell are recorded and stored in our brain as memories.

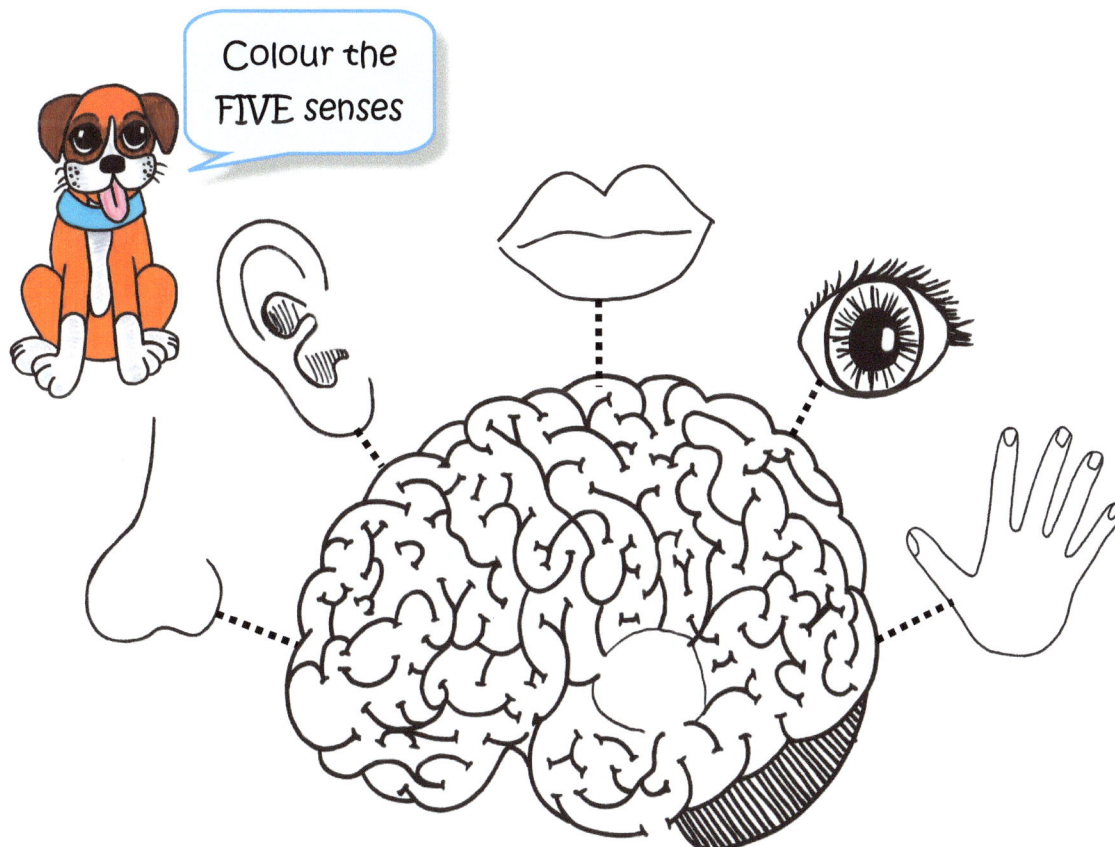

Colour the
FIVE senses

MEMORY MAKING

Benson had so many great times with Lucy. Each day his senses made memories of the fun times they had together!

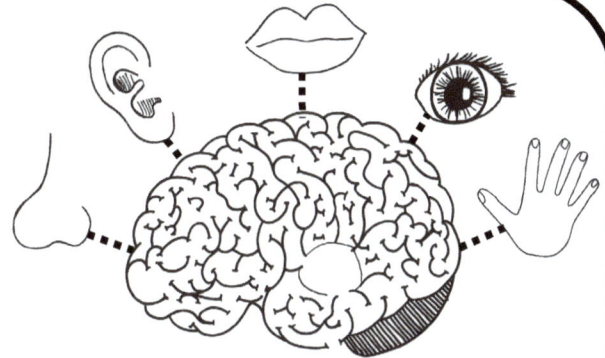

Draw in the box something Benson remembered **SEEING** with Lucy?

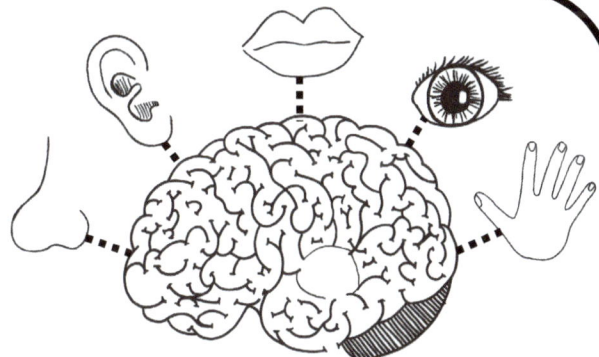

Circle and colour the correct sense

Draw in the box something Benson remembered **HEARING** with Lucy?

Circle and colour the correct sense

84

Draw in the box something Benson remembered **FEELING** with Lucy?

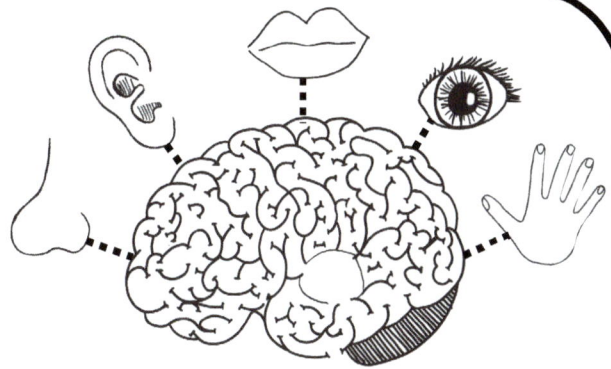

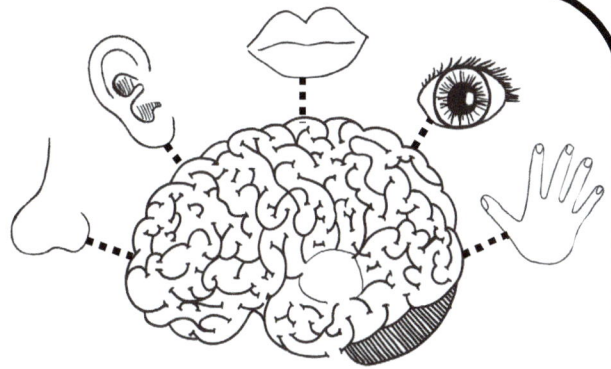

Circle and colour the correct sense

Draw in the box something Benson remembered **SMELLING** with Lucy?

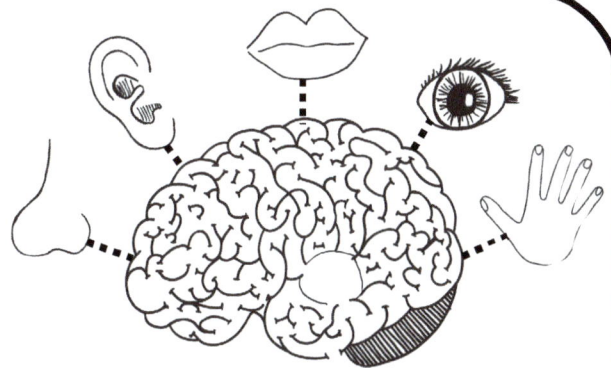

Circle and colour the correct sense

Draw in the box something Benson remembered **TASTING** with Lucy?

Circle and colour the correct sense

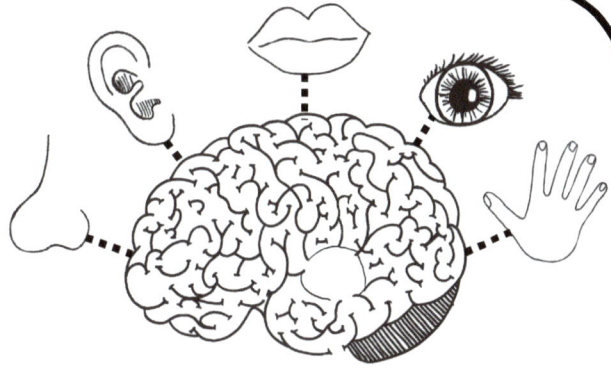

Draw in the box something Benson remembered **FEELING** with Lucy?

Circle and colour the correct sense

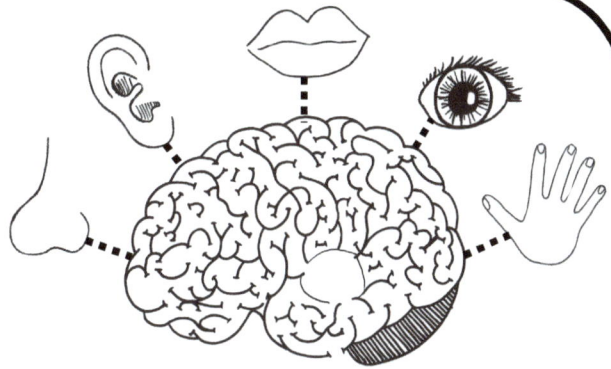

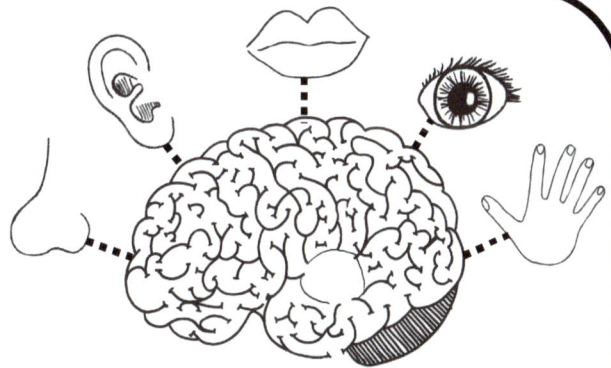

Draw in the box something Benson remembered **SMELLING** with Lucy?

Circle and colour the correct sense

Draw in the box something Benson remembered **TASTING** with Lucy?

Circle and colour the correct sense

88

Read and colour the words that describe how Benson felt after Lucy's accident. In the CIRCLE draw a face to show what each word looks like.

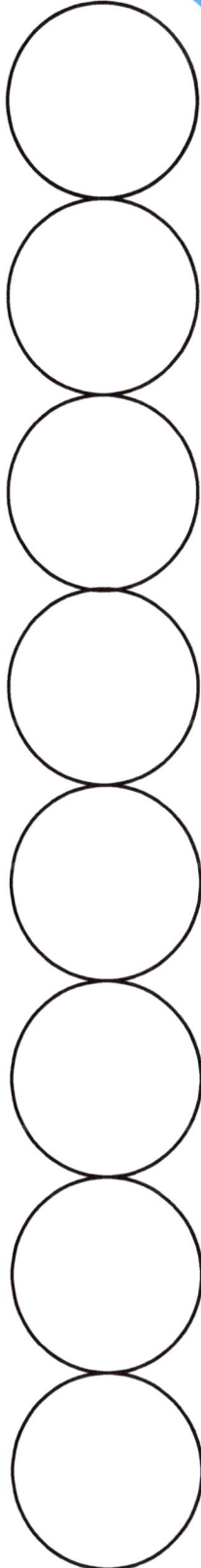

SAD

unhappy

SCARED

AFRAID

WORRIED

ANGRY

Yukky

Down

90

Benson is feeling MISERABLE! Help him find his bone

Where is my bone?

START

FRAMING BENSON'S FEARS

Benson remembered the day of Lucy's accident. In the picture frames, draw Benson's bad, sad and scary memories.

Colour in the frames!

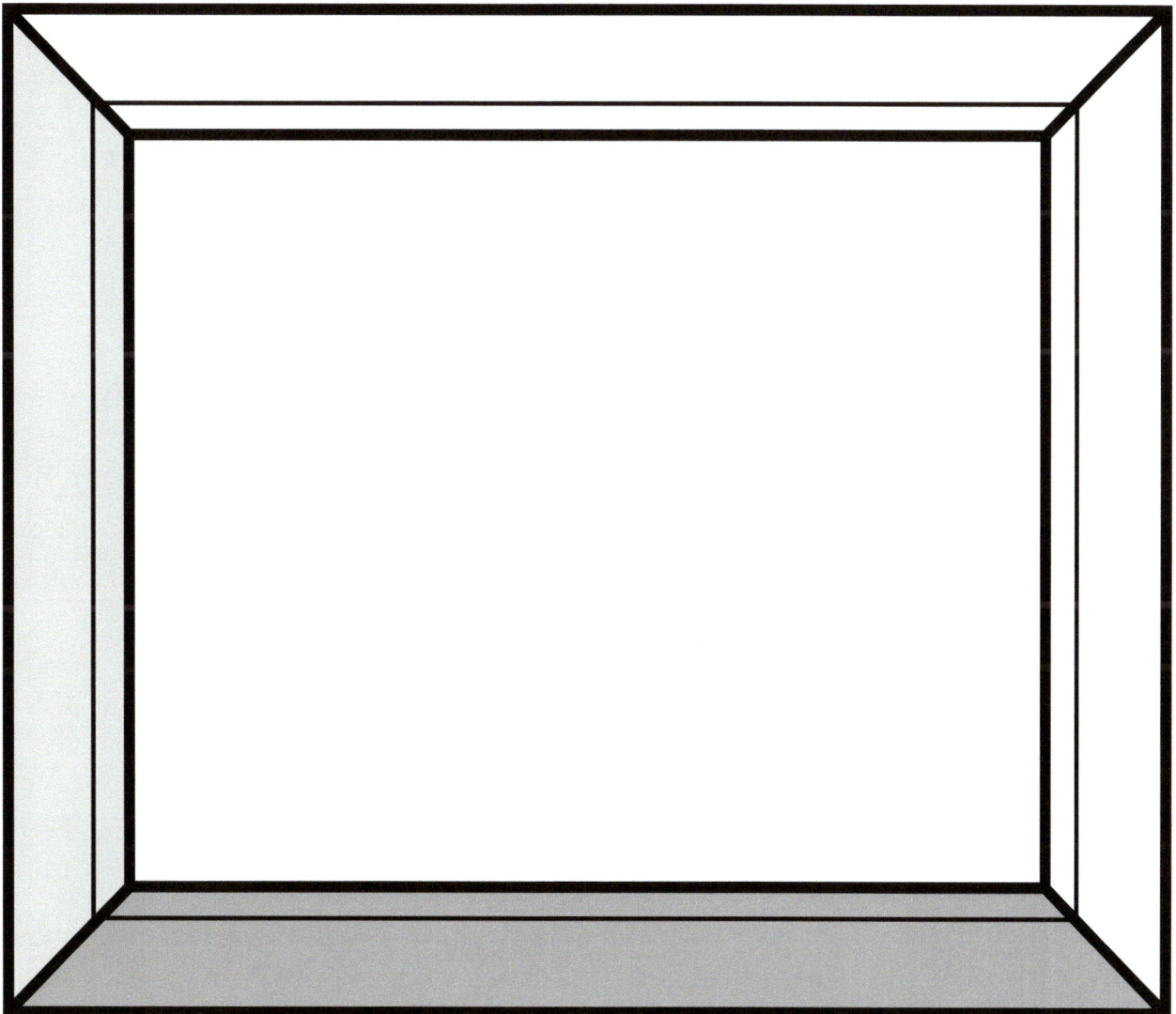

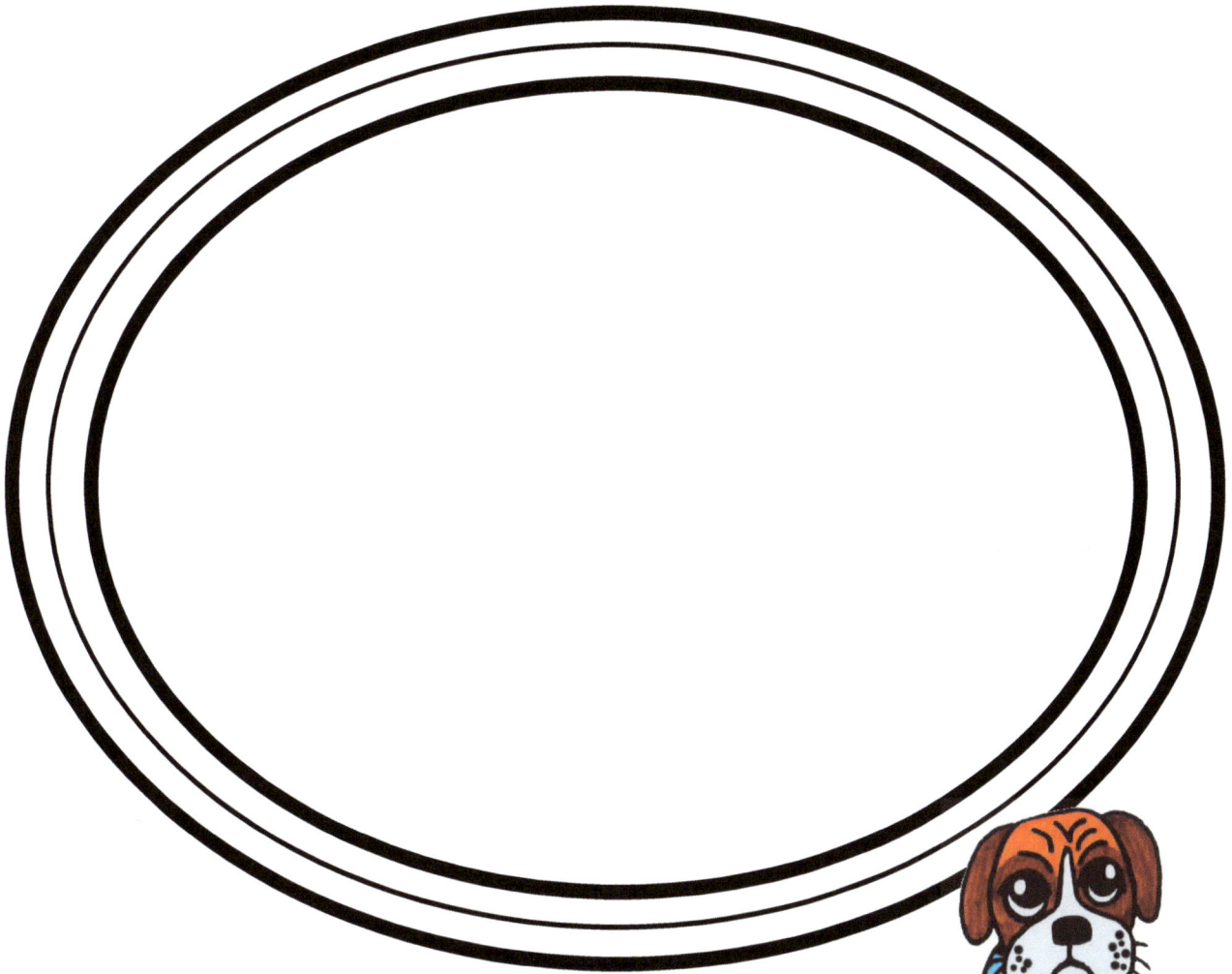

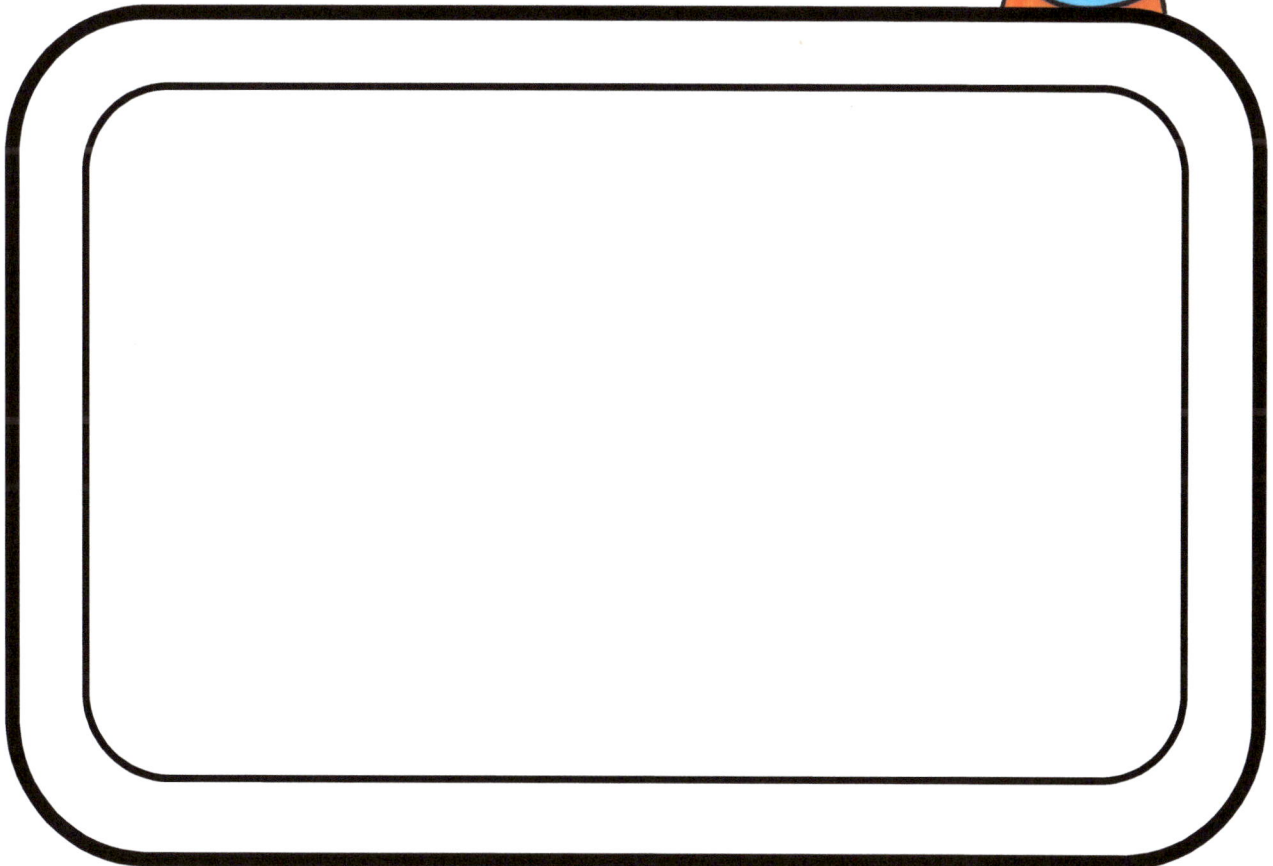

96

FRAMING MY FEARS

Children also remember many things that frighten them. In the picture frames, draw any bad, sad or scary memories a child might have.

Colour in the frames as well!

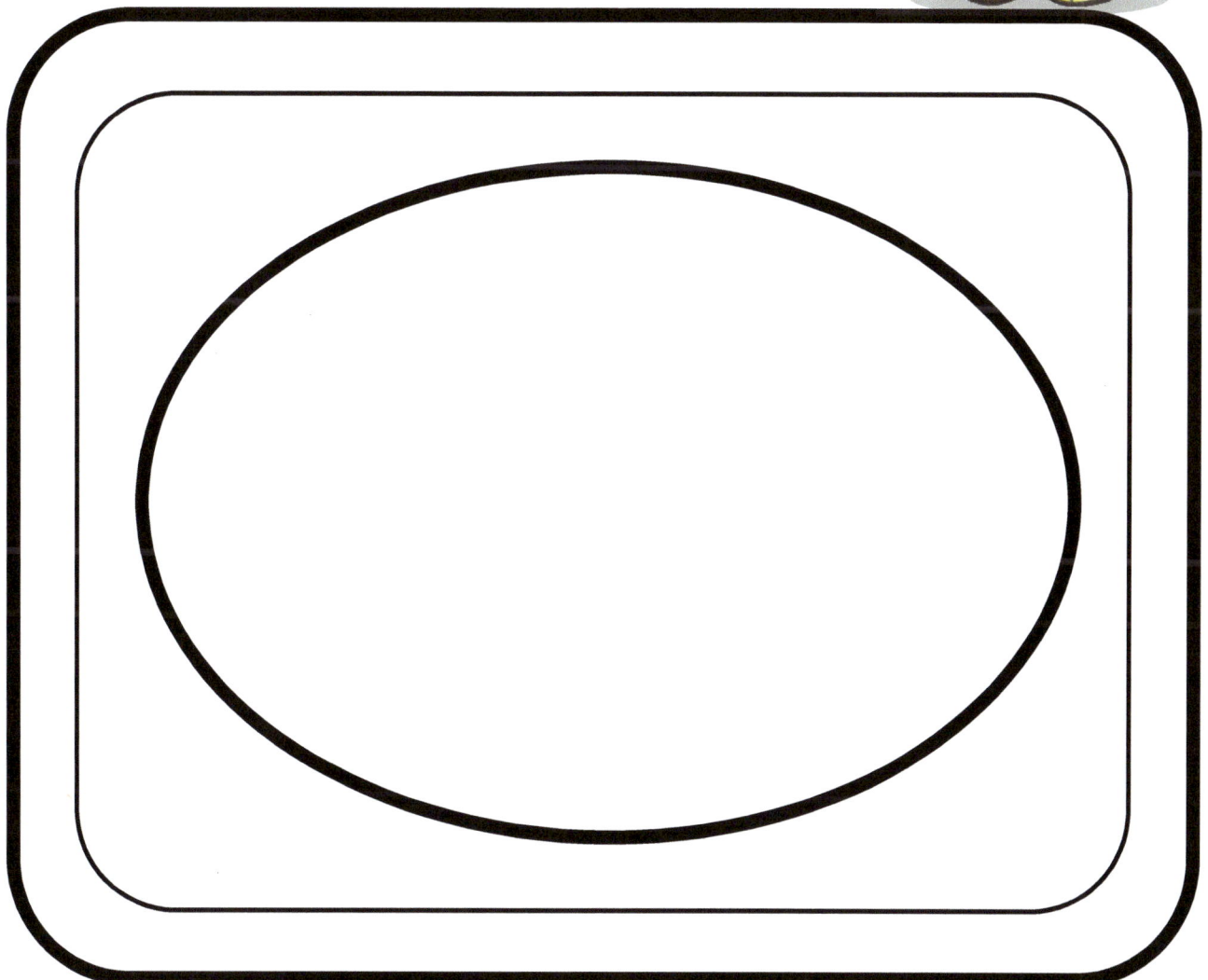

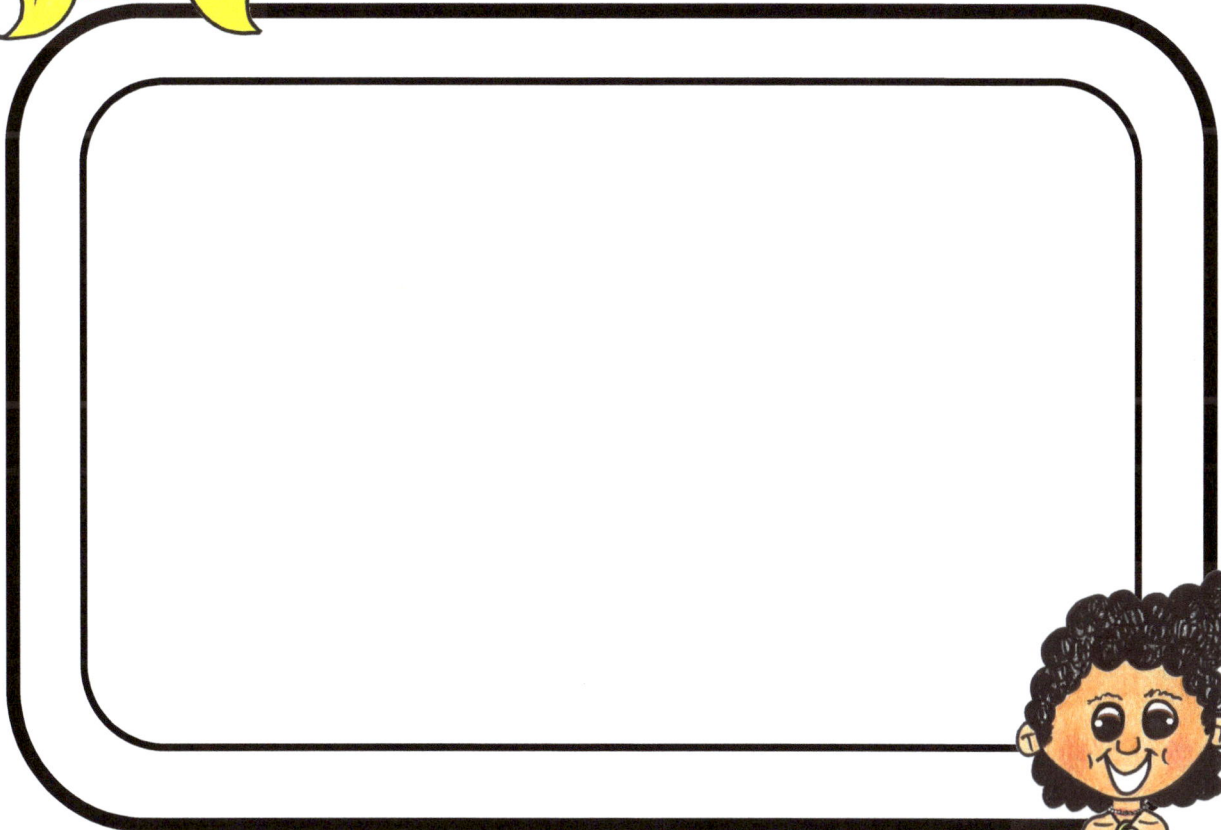

100

BENSON'S FEAR RESPONSES

How did being frightened and sad feel inside Benson's body? Circle any of the feelings Benson felt.

Benson wants to party

Benson feels happy

Benson wants to be with his friends

Benson feels sad

Benson's tummy hurts

Benson has the wiggles

Benson is excited!

Benson feels like playing

Benson is panting

Benson feels miserable

Benson feels tired

Benson feels sick

Benson's heart is beating fast

Benson has sore muscles

Benson feels peaceful

Benson feels up-side down

BAD, SAD & SCARY RESPONSES

How does being frightened, sad or angry feel inside your body? Circle how you feel.

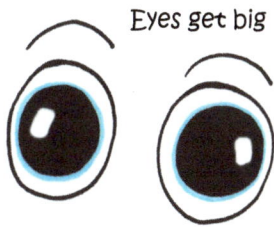

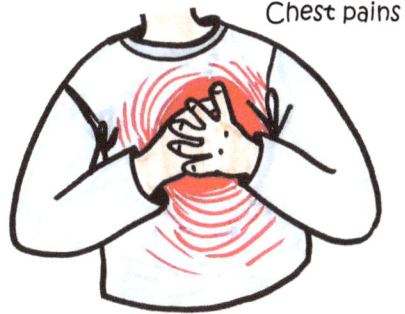

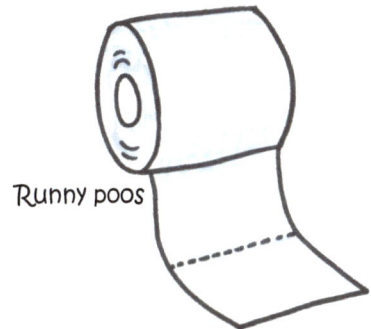

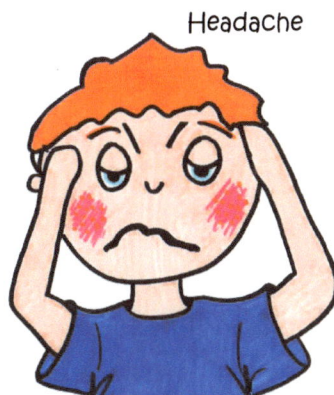

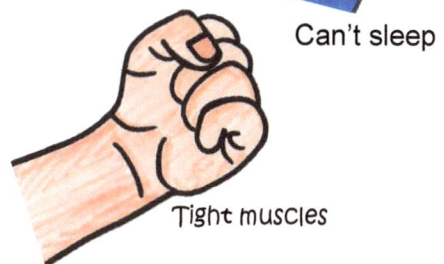

Eyes get big

Heart beats fast

Chest pains

Tummy feels sore

Sweaty

Dry mouth

Runny poos

Tired

Can't sleep

Sick

Headache

Tight muscles

BENSON'S HIDING PLACES

Draw the places I hid when I was frightened.
The first one is done for you.

MY HIDING PLACES

Where would you hide if you were frightened?

Draw what I'm hiding under.

STORM OF FEAR

When something bad, sad or scary happens it can feel like we are caught in a terrible STORM.
What do you do and where do you go when the storm of fear is around you?
Circle the raindrops or add your own ideas.

hide away

read a book to forget

run away

go to sleep

talk to someone

get angry

become very sad

WHEN LIFE CHANGES

Sometimes things happen that we cannot control. On those days everything about our life can change.

The pictures below show children who have had their lives changed because of something bad, sad or scary.

Draw lines to match the picture with the words to explain what has happened to the children

	This boy's daddy died of cancer.
	This little girl had an accident and is no longer able to walk.
	Fires destroyed this girl's home and everything she owned.
	This family no longer is able to live together.

In each of the pictures, the children have LOST SOMETHING SPECIAL. Can you identify what it is? *(Discuss this with an adult)*

When bad, sad or scary things happen to us it can change...

what we do
where we go
how we live.

It is normal to want things to be the same. Sometimes this can't happen.

The children in the pictures had their lives changed forever. Each child needed to make a choice.

What choice should they make???

Draw a BIG CIRCLE around the best choice.

CHOICE ONE
The child could feel there is no way out. They could feel trapped.

CHOICE TWO
The child could talk with someone they trust. They could begin to think of new ideas and new plans.

Benson is STUCK!

Benson doesn't want to go out and play any more. He doesn't want to leave the house. He is worried about everything!

Benson is too sad and frightened to want to do things he used to enjoy.

Benson talked with Uncle Boris. He chose to...
> **get up**
> > **get out**
> > > **get going!**

He chose to have fun and enjoy life again.

Draw ME jumping out of the box!

BENSON IS TRAPPED

Help me find my way out from my hiding place

MOVING FORWARD

THINGS TO REMEMBER

1. Accidents sometimes just happen, even when we do safe things to help protect us.

2. Bad, sad or scary experiences are usually not your fault

3. It is normal to feel anxious or sad after something bad, sad or scary has happened.

Write on each finger someone you trust who you could talk to

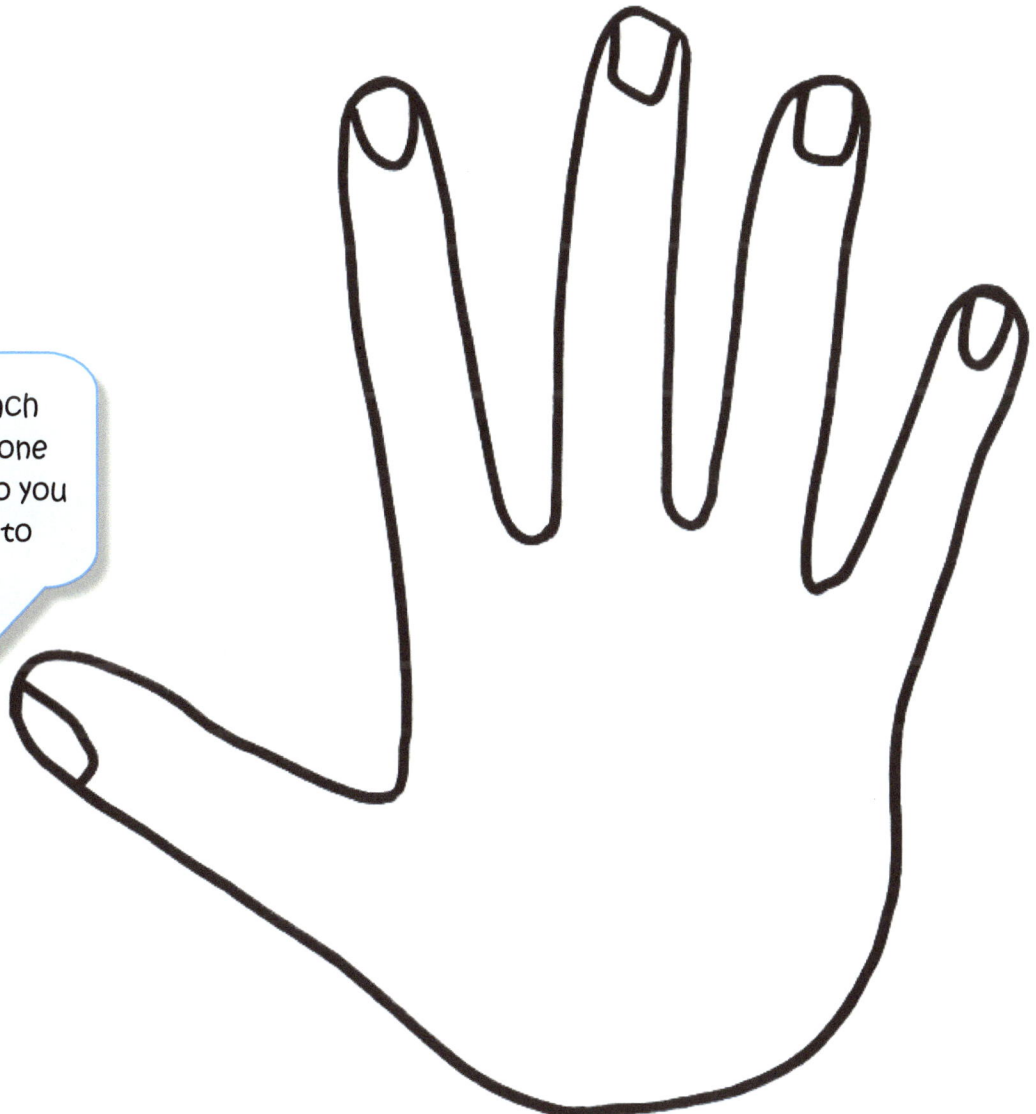

Colour the words that describe how Benson wanted to feel again. In the circle draw a face to show what each word looks like.

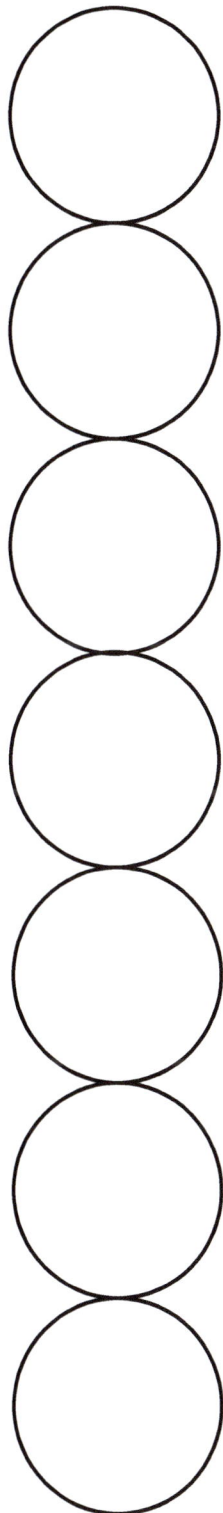

Happy

playful

EXITED

energised

BoUnCy

BRAVE

calm

BUCKET OF BALLOONS

Running with
Uncle Boris

I talked
with
Uncle Boris

The balloons show
TWO things Benson
did to help him get
well.

Draw or write
other ideas for
Benson in the
empty balloons.

BOUQUET OF BALLOONS

I could pick flowers for someone

MY BOUQUET TO SHARE

Being with people I trust helps me to feel well again. It is called **connecting**.

In the balloons draw other ways to **connect** with:

- family
- carers
- friends
- school mates
- teachers
- neighbours
- pets
- others

126

WORDS OF WELLNESS

```
F T V B R A V E X C S C
R E T A L K S E V O H E
I R G D Q Y P N H O A M
E R M Z L W R J A L R B
N I G R E A T O P P E W
D F J P L A Y Y P S R V
S I N T T Y O D Y K L S
A C J O Y G O O D H R X
```

BRAVE

COOL

ENJOY

FRIENDS

GOOD

GREAT

JOY

PLAY

SHARE

TALK

TERRIFIC

Find the following words in the puzzle. Words are hidden ➡ and ⬇

128

HIDDEN WORDS

Find the words hidden in the picture

HAPPY FUN PLAYFUL EXCITED SAFE CALM BRAVE

This is to certify that

has successfully completed

**THE BENSON THE BOXER
JUNIOR WORKSHEETS
on
LOSS AND LIFE**

DATE:

ANSWER PAGE

WORDS OF WELLNESS
ANSWERS

F	T	V	B	R	A	V	E	X	C	S	C
R	E	T	A	L	K	S	E	V	O	H	E
I	R	G	D	Q	Y	P	N	H	O	A	M
E	R	M	Z	L	W	R	J	A	L	R	B
N	I	G	R	E	A	T	O	P	P	E	W
D	F	J	P	L	A	Y	Y	P	S	R	X
S	I	N	T	T	Y	O	D	Y	K	L	S
A	C	J	O	Y	G	O	O	D	H	R	X

BRAVE
COOL
ENJOY
FRIENDS
GOOD
GREAT
JOY
PLAY
SHARE
TALK
TERRIFIC

Find the following words in the puzzle. Words are hidden → and ↓

BENSON IS TRAPPED
ANSWERS

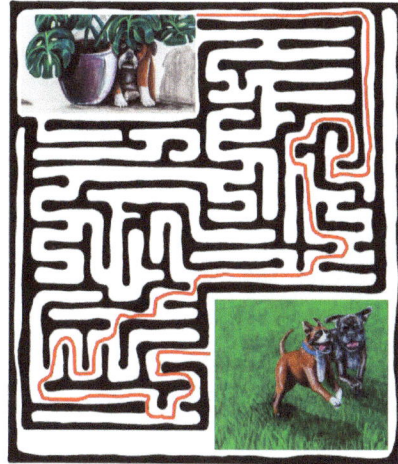

HIDDEN WORDS ANSWERS
Find the words hidden in the picture

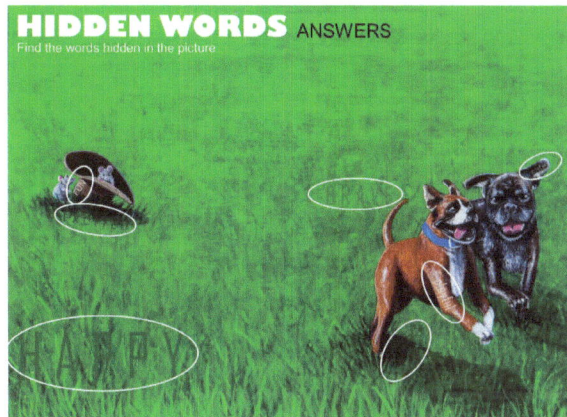

HAPPY FUN PLAYFUL EXCITED SAFE CALM BRAVE

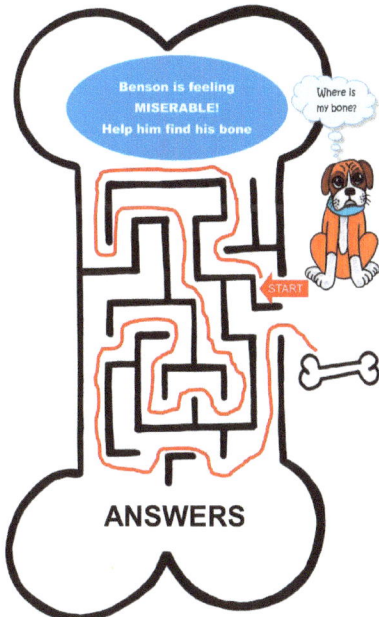

Benson is feeling MISERABLE! Help him find his bone

Where is my bone?

START

ANSWERS

WHEN LIFE CHANGES

Sometimes things happen that we cannot control. On those days everything about our life can change.

The pictures below show children who have had their lives changed because of something bad, sad or scary.

Draw lines to match the picture with the words to explain what has happened to the children

This boy's daddy died of cancer.

This little girl had an accident and is no longer able to walk.

Fires destroyed this girl's home and everything she owned.

This family no longer is able to live together.

In each of the pictures, the children have LOST SOMETHING SPECIAL. Can you identify what it is? *(Discuss this with an adult)*

SENIOR
WORKBOOK

For Ages 8-12

CONTENTS

Hi there!

Hi there kids,

Welcome to **Benson the Boxer** Workbook!

This workbook is created and designed just for you! It is a workbook full of colourful, fun and interesting activities. It is also a book of learning. The activities will help explain why you feel the way you do when something bad, sad or scary happens. But, the most important part of this workbook, is that it gives ideas on how to feel better right now and whenever your feel scared or sad again in the future.

This book is so cool! The activities are heaps of fun! However, if at any time you feel a little uncomfortable, find someone you trust to talk to. Your feelings are normal and sharing with someone you trust will calm your fears and will help you feel safe and in control of the things that have frightened you or made you sad.

I'm so glad you are joining me on the journey to living a life of fun and wellness...

Let's begin!

Benson

Read and colour the words that describe how Benson felt after Lucy's accident. In the circle draw a face to show what each word looks like.

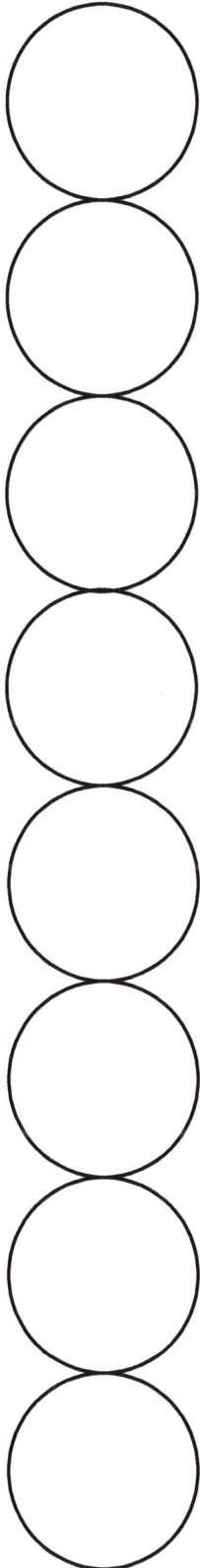

SAD

miserable

SCARED

NERVOUS

WORRIED

ANGRY

Gloomy

D E Pressed

142

FRAMING our FEARS

We all experience things that frighten us or make us sad. In the frames below, DRAW things that may be bad, sad or scary.

Colour in the frames!

BENSON'S BAROMETER OF FEAR

How frightened was Benson when he was lost in the bush?

NOT VERY SCARED   SCARED   REALLY SCARED

Draw what I did even though I was scared

How frightened was Benson when he faced the group of angry bullies?

NOT VERY SCARED   SCARED   REALLY SCARED

Draw what I did even though I was scared

BENSON'S BAROMETER OF FEAR

How frightened was Benson when he saw
something really sad happen to Lucy?

NOT VERY SCARED   SCARED   REALLY SCARED

Draw what I did after the accident

How frightened was Benson when he heard a
BANG, a CRASH, a THUD or a POP?

NOT VERY SCARED   SCARED   REALLY SCARED

Draw where else I hid

BENSON'S FEAR RESPONSES

How did being frightened and sad feel inside Benson's body? Circle any of the feelings Benson felt.

Benson feels happy

Benson wants to be with his friends

Benson feels sad

Benson wants to party

Benson's tummy hurts

Benson has the wiggles

Benson is excited!

Benson's breathing is fast

Benson feels like playing

Benson feels miserable

Benson feels sick. He wants to vomit

Benson feels tired. He can't sleep

Benson's heart is beating fast

Benson feels peaceful

Benson feels up-side down

BAD, SAD & SCARY RESPONSES

How does being frightened, sad or angry feel inside your body? Circle the feelings that apply to you.

Eyes get bigger as pupils dilate

Heart beats faster

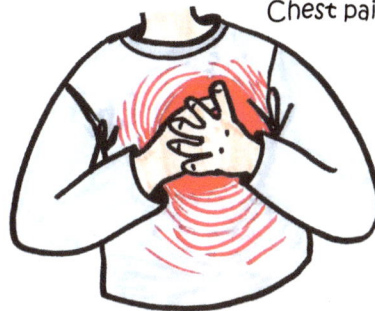

Chest pains

Stomach feels tight and knotty

Sweating or feeling chilled

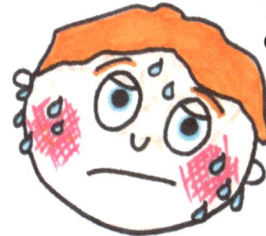

Dry mouth

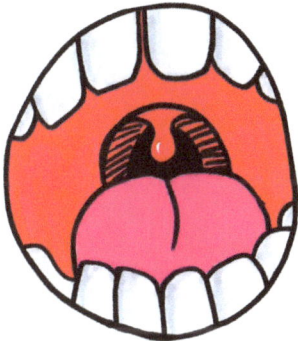

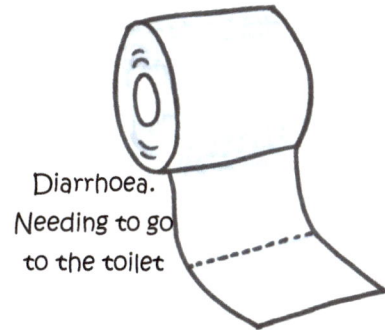

Diarrhoea. Needing to go to the toilet

Exhaustion

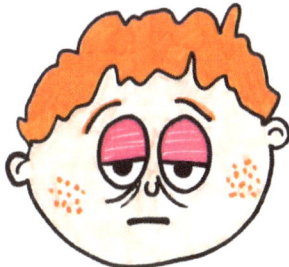

Nausea - feeling you want to vomit

Headache

Muscles become tense

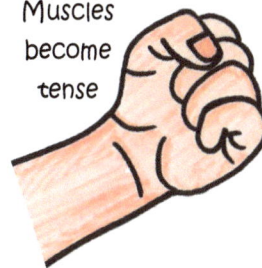

Can't sleep or relax

152

MEMORY MAKING

Our brain records memories that we receive from our senses.

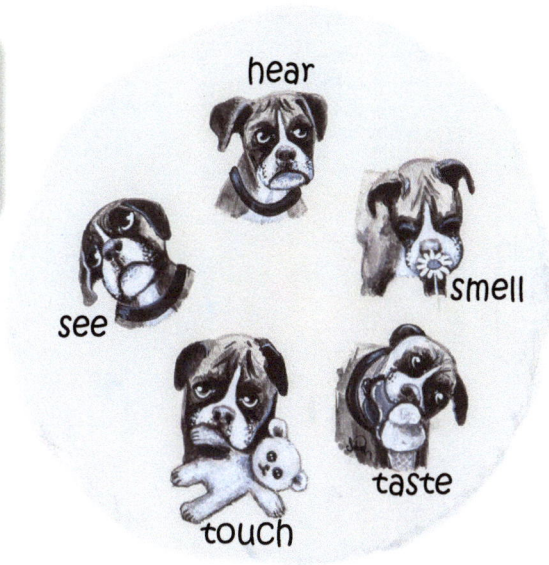

hear

see

smell

touch

taste

Most of the time our brain receives safe and happy messages from things that we touch, smell, taste, see and hear. These sensory messages are stored in the network of our brain as memories.

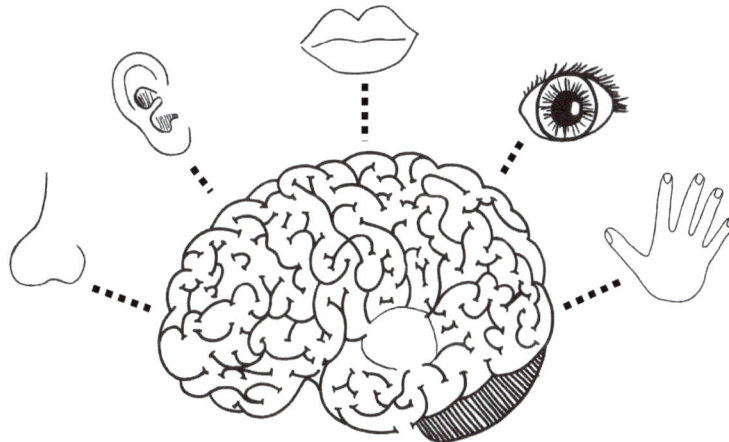

Our brain also receives messages that startle and alarm us. We may hear something that frightens us, we might see something scary, we could smell something dangerous, we could taste something yukky, or we might experience a touch that hurts or that makes us feel uncomfortable.

When Benson witnessed Lucy's terrible accident many of his sense were alerted and the MEMORIES were stored in his brain.

What did Benson remember *seeing*? ....

What did Benson remember *hearing*? ....

What did Benson *feel*? ....

154

BRAIN MAZE

156

INSTRUCTIONS: Make your way through the BRAIN MAZE to find out what helped Benson move forward.

CAUTION! You will need to navigate your way around Amy G'dala. Amy and her twin sister are always on the alert, sensing every danger. Be brave and keep going!

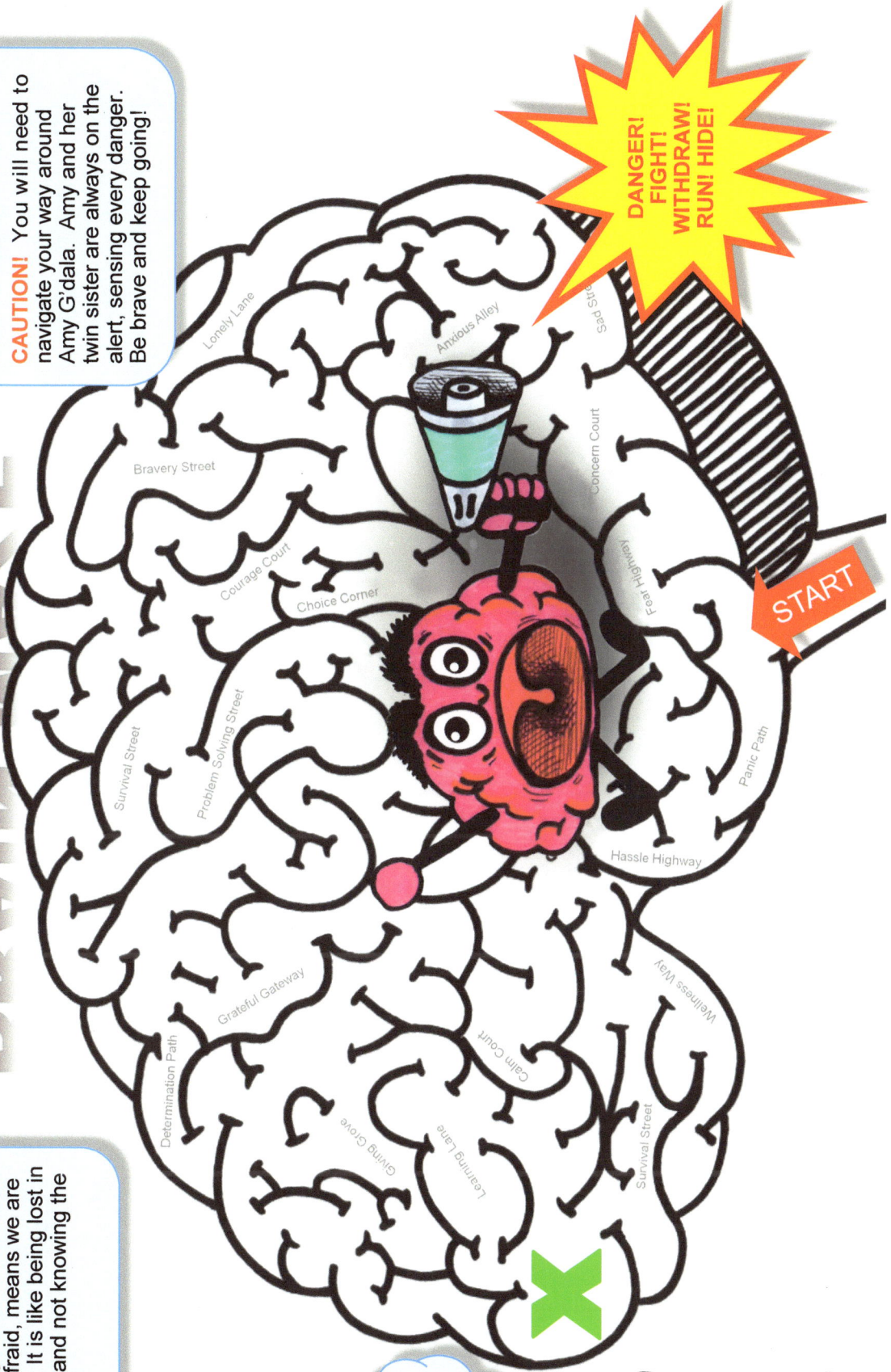

Benson's fear meant he stopped doing the things he used to enjoy. Doing nothing and going nowhere, because we are afraid, means we are trapped. It is like being lost in a **MAZE** and not knowing the way out!

DANGER!
FIGHT!
WITHDRAW!
RUN! HIDE!

START

Lonely Lane
Anxious Alley
Sad Str
Bravery Street
Concern Court
Courage Court
Choice Corner
Fear Highway
Panic Path
Survival Street
Problem Solving Street
Hassle Highway
Determination Path
Grateful Gateway
Calm Court
Wellness Way
Giving Grove
Learning Lane
Survival Street

Surviving and thriving!

Bensons FEAR BOX

Benson's fears affected every part of his life and also the lives of others around him.

He didn't feel like talking. He just wanted to be alone. He didn't want to play anymore!

It was as if Benson was **STUCK IN A BOX** doing nothing, going nowhere but still feeling **MISERABLE!**

What did Benson stop doing when he became afraid?

....

....

How did Benson's fears affect his friends and others around him?

....

....

STORM OF FEAR

WHAT I DO WHEN I'M SCARED, SAD OR UPSET?

When something bad, sad or scary happens it can feel like we are caught in a terrible STORM. Each raindrop tells us some things we might do when we are scared, sad or upset. Colour blue the raindrops you would choose. Use the blank raindrops to add your own ideas.

hide away

find someone to help me

run away

go to a friends house

go to sleep

get angry

curl up in a ball

play recklessly

become very sad

read a book to forget

FACING THE
MAZE
OF
UNCERTAINTY

Benson feels lonely and would love to play ball with Lucy again. Follow the maze to see if Benson can connect with Lucy.

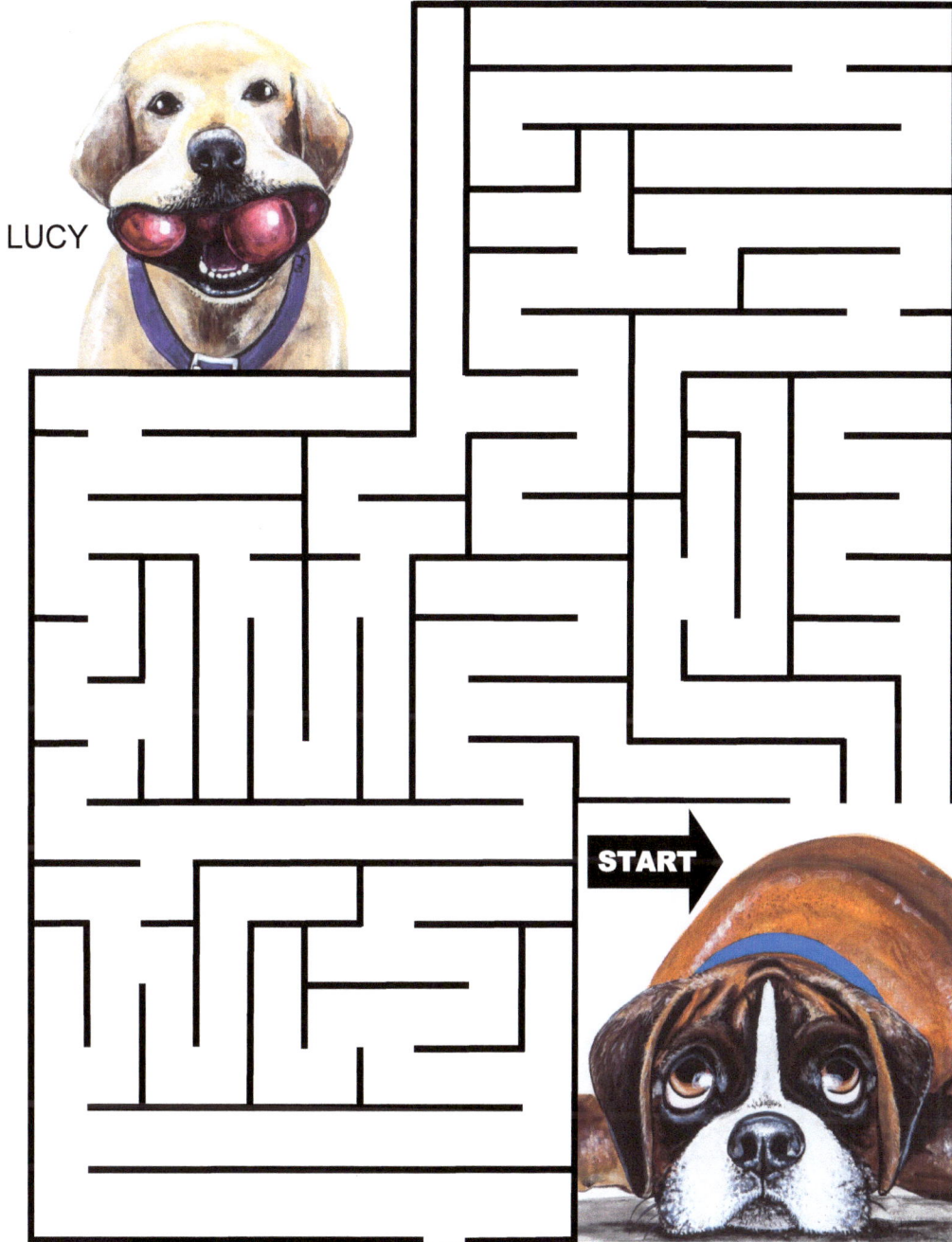

LUCY

START

There are always other options when our way is blocked. Who can Benson now connect with when he feels lonely?

FACING THE MAZE OF UNCERTAINTY

When we experience something bad, sad or scary our world can be turned completely upside down!

We desperately try to change the situation, to have things back how they used to be. But just like Benson discovered in the MAZE OF UNCERTAINTY, trying to have what he used to have sent him straight into a dead end!
To play ball with Lucy again was not going to happen, sadly she was gone.

UPSIDE DOWN!

164

There are things that happen in the world that we cannot control.
On those days - everything about our life can change.

Above are pictures of children who have had their lives changed because of a situation they couldn't control.

Write in the boxes what you think has happened to the children in the pictures?

Unexpected situations can change...
what we do
where we go
how we live.
It is normal to want to have things back as they were before, but the more we try, the more we hit a **DEAD-END** in the **MAZE** of **LIFE**.

We end up feeling trapped and there is no way out!!

166

MOVING FORWARD

THINGS TO REMEMBER

1. Accidents happen - It is impossible to be protected from everything, even when we take precautions to help keep safe.

2. Realise that a bad, sad or scary experience is not usually your fault.

3. Feeling, sad, miserable, anxious and fearful are normal re actions after something bad, sad or scary has happened.

Write on each finger someone you trust who you could talk to

168

MOVING FORWARD

Positive things to do:

1. Connect with someone.

2. Take a step or two back, breathe deeply, consider the options and look for an alternative path.

Different takes getting used to - but it's not necessarily bad!

Change is not easy - but things can work out OK! Moving on to PLAN B - means you don't get to do PLAN A, but you can still have a good plan!

In other words - try something different!

~~PLAN A~~

PLAN B

COLOUR **GREEN** the brain smart things to do when you feel trapped.

COLOUR **RED** the activities that stop you moving forward.

Exercise - walking , playing, running and jumping	Stay alone and don't talk to anyone
Do something to yourself that causes more pain or fear	Connect with someone - make a phone call, send a txt, connect on Facebook
Run away and hide	Wrap yourself in a soft blanket and read a book that you can tell others about
Get busy - do something you love to do	Stay at home and watch TV shows
Do fun activities with your friends - like riding bikes, hiking or playing sport	Draw or write about your thoughts (journaling)
Breathe deeply and practice mindfulness	Think of something to be grateful for
Sing - it calms you and drives away fear and anxiety	Talk to someone you trust - nothing is so awful that we can't talk to someone about it
Play computer games all day	Get angry because things have not turned out how they should have

STEPS TO WELLNESS

1. Take small steps by first connecting to someone you can trust. Uncle Boris encouraged Benson to take small steps to reach out and connect with others

Benson connected with Uncle Boris

Draw or write people I can connect with:

2. When you feel safe and ready talk about each memory that is bad, sad or scary.

Lucy running after the ball

Playing with Lucy

Playing in the park - running and jumping

Bensons memories of the scary day

Lucy running after the ball

The ball bouncing onto the road

Playing with a bouncy ball

My memories of something bad, sad or scary.

3. Look closely at the memory - is it still a danger and unsafe?

Scary!

Playing in the park - running and jumping	SAFE
Playing with Lucy	SAFE
Playing with a bouncy ball	SAFE
The ball bouncing onto the road	UNSAFE
Lucy running onto the road	UNSAFE

Benson's safe and unsafe memories

My safe and unsafe memories:

4. Sometimes memories need to be discarded because they are no longer useful.

Memories that are no longer useful for Benson:

- Being frightened of car and trucks
- Being scared of bouncing balls
- Feeling guilty that it was his fault the accident happened
- Wishing he could have made Lucy stop!

Memories that are no longer useful for me:

5. Pack the memories you want to keep in boxes, which are like memory compartments.

The memories Benson wants to keep

The memories I want to keep

6. GET UP, GET OUT and GET GOING!
Even if what you do now is different.

Start to move forward by getting out
and doing the things you used to enjoy,
even if what you do is going to now be
different.

Lucy is no longer outside the window waiting for
Benson, but what else could Benson see?

....

....

What could he still enjoy doing?

....

....

What is outside of your window?

What could you still enjoy?

Draw
here

Forest of Fear

NUMBER of PLAYERS

Two, Three or Four

OBJECT of THE GAME

Finish the game to become a **CHAMPION** of awesome decisions whenever something bad, sad or scary happens.

EQUIPMENT NEEDED

1 dice

1 container for shaking the dice

1 counter/marker for each player'

1 playing board

HOW to PLAY

1 Players take turns to roll a dice and move through The Forest of Fear. The person to start is the person who throws the highest number when rolling the dice.

2 Move the counter forward the number of spaces shown on your throw of the dice.

3 When players land on a space containing words, they must follow the instructions stated.

4 Players are able to occupy the same space at the same time.

Everyone who finishes the game is a **CHAMPION!**

The Forest

Start

1

2 Someone hurts your feelings. You run and hide. Miss ONE turn

3

4 You weren't invited to a party. You decide to bake cookies for your neighbour. Jump forward TWO spaces

10

11

12 Your friends tease you about having your hair cut. You laugh it off instead of getting angry. Jump forward ONE space

13

19

20 You broke your arm and cut your knee when you fell off your bike. You decide it's too dangerous to ever ride a bike ever again. Move back THREE spaces

21

22

28 You were really scared when you saw a snake in the back-yard. You decide to not go out and play again. Miss TWO turns

29

30 You fail a test and decide to study harder next time. Jump forward ONE space.

31

6 · 7 · 8 You felt embarrassed when you had to do a school talk. You ran out of the room. Miss TWO turns · 9

15 · 16 You didn't study for an important school test. You decide to just stay home so you can miss it. Move back TWO spaces · 17 · 18 You see something bad happen on the way home from school. You decide to talk to an adult you trust about it. Jump forward TWO spaces

24 You get lost in the shopping centre. You go and ask a shop owner for help. Jump forward ONE space · 25 · 26 · 27

33 · 34 You are not picked to play on a sports team. You decide to invite someone over to play with your toys. Jump forward ONE space · 35 · 36 YOU ARE A CHAMPION! YOU have made awesome decisions when something BAD, SAD or SCARY happens

182

THE GAME

is a

GAME of CHANCE

How you move through the game depends on your roll of the dice. You are considered lucky if you land on a number that lets you quickly move ahead. It is considered unlucky of you land on a number that tells you to go back.

The game is a representation of life, but
LIFE IS NOT A GAME OF CHANCE
We make choices every day.

When something bad, sad or scary happens,
WE MAKE CHOICES how we will react.

The next page gives ideas to move forward when something bad, sad or scary happens.

The best thing to do is to make a choice to connect with someone.

Hello

183

BOUQUET OF BALLOONS

Send a text message to a friend to say "hi"

Make a card for someone who's not feeling so good

Invite someone over to play

Build a cubby house

Take your dog for a run

Help someone in your neighbourhood

Go to a movie with a friend

Take a ride on your bike

Play sport with your friends

IDEAS TO MOVE FORWARD

Reach out to others with a BOUQUET OF BALLOONS.

Which balloons could you pull down so that you can connect with someone else.

Finish colouring the balloons of the things you could do.

Draw other balloons with more ideas.

Can you think of other balloons you to add?

184

Colour the words that describe how Benson wanted to feel again. In the circle draw a face to show what each word looks like.

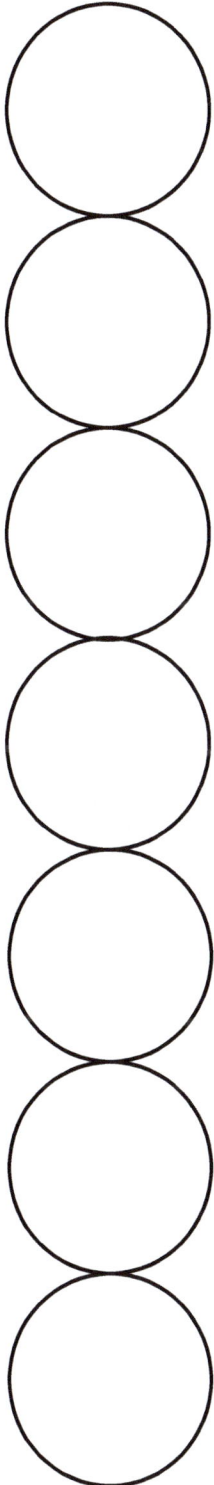

Happy

playful

EXITED

motivated

BoUnCy

BRAVE

calm

186

Colour in the clouds that tell of the happy things Benson remembered

Rolling on his back and laughing out loud

Riding in the car feeling the breeze on his face

Talking with farmyard friends

Hiding under the couch

Sitting by the door missing Lucy

Eating delicious bones

Playing with the ball

Staying inside the house

188

SURVIVING TO THRIVING

```
M O T I V A T E O H E L P B X A E Z
B S A J Y M I F C R E A T E S N N L
Z U U C M X E N R C E S A S I M C I
F P Y R O O X S V I H F S S I U O S
U P N R V M V S S E E E I K Y P U T
X O P U S I F E P A N N E C M L R E
N R P N M O V O S K G T D R N I A P
C T S E I L Q E R V N E D S P F G S
E O G C L W J V A T E S R K H T E U
N H L O E K P R C O N N E C T I Y K
W L M P H I N S P I R E P L A Y P V
C B U I L D X T H R I V E K R L F D
```

BUILD   MOTIVATE

CHEER   MOVE

COMFORT   PLAY

CONNECT   RUN

CREATE   SMILE

ENCOURAGE   STEPS

FRIENDSHIP   SUPPORT

HELP   SURVIVE

INSPIRE   THRIVE

INVENT   UPLIFT

MESSAGE

Find the following words in the puzzle. Words are hidden → ↓ and ↘

190

© Cortxion, 2018

QUIZ

peekaboo

Let's see what do you remember about trauma. What do you notice in your body when you feel frightened?

1. Name **FOUR** signs of being frightened

2. What can **YOU** do when you are afraid?

3. Name something you could do if you **see** something bad, sad or scary	
Name something you could do if you **hear** something bad, sad or scary	
Name something you could do if you **smell** something bad, sad or scary	
Name something you could do if you **touch** something bad, sad or scary	
Name something you could do if you **taste** something bad, sad or scary	
Name something you could do if someone **does something** bad, sad or scary to **YOU**	
4. Who can help you when you feel frightened?	

5. Jesse gasps and stands frozen as he sees a SNAKE slither under the log he is about to step over. He screams loudly and his mum comes running with a stick to scare the snake away. What should Jesse do next?

Go into the house, shut himself in his room and never play outside again so that the snake can't get him.	Remain playing outside, but ensure he is playing with shoes on and not near any dead logs or in log grass	Continue playing where he saw the snake and not take care to ensure safety

6. Ryan was walking home from school when he was stopped by THREE BOYS. They started to threaten him and call him names. They pushed him out of the way then let him run home. What should Ryan do next?

Stay home from school and never go back again	Talk to someone he trusts about the incident and ask for help	Push the boys back, call them names and start to fight again

192

This is to certify that

has successfully completed

**THE BENSON THE BOXER
SENIOR WORKSHEETS
on
LOSS AND LIFE**

DATE:

ANSWERS

SURVIVING TO THRIVING

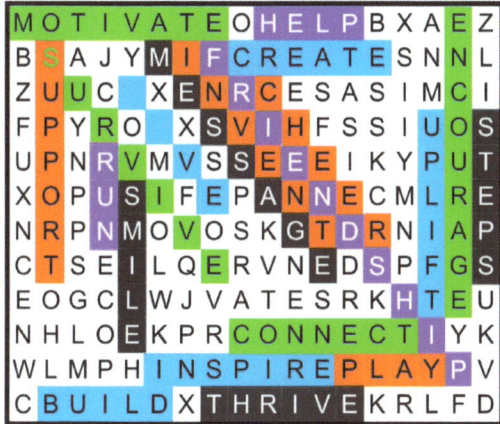

M	O	T	I	V	A	T	E	O	H	E	L	P	B	X	A	E	Z
B	S	A	J	Y	M	I	F	C	R	E	A	T	E	S	N	N	L
Z	U	U	C	X	E	N	R	C	E	S	A	S	I	M	C	I	
F	P	Y	R	O	X	S	V	I	H	F	S	S	I	U	O	S	
U	P	N	R	V	M	V	S	S	E	E	E	I	K	Y	P	U	T
X	O	P	U	S	I	F	E	P	A	N	N	E	C	M	L	R	E
N	R	P	N	M	O	V	O	S	K	G	T	D	R	N	I	A	P
C	T	S	E	I	L	Q	E	R	V	N	E	D	S	P	F	G	S
E	O	G	C	L	W	J	V	A	T	E	S	R	K	H	T	E	U
N	H	L	O	E	K	P	R	C	O	N	N	E	C	T	I	Y	K
W	L	M	P	H	I	N	S	P	I	R	E	P	L	A	Y	P	V
C	B	U	I	L	D	X	T	H	R	I	V	E	K	R	L	F	D

BUILD   MOTIVATE
CHEER   MOVE
COMFORT   PLAY
CONNECT   RUN
CREATE   SMILE
ENCOURAGE   STEPS
FRIENDSHIP   SUPPORT
HELP   SURVIVE
INSPIRE   THRIVE
INVENT   UPLIFT
MESSAGE

FACING THE MAZE OF UNCERTAINTY
ANSWER PAGE

Benson feels lonely and would love to play ball with Lucy again. Follow the maze to see if Benson can connect with Lucy.

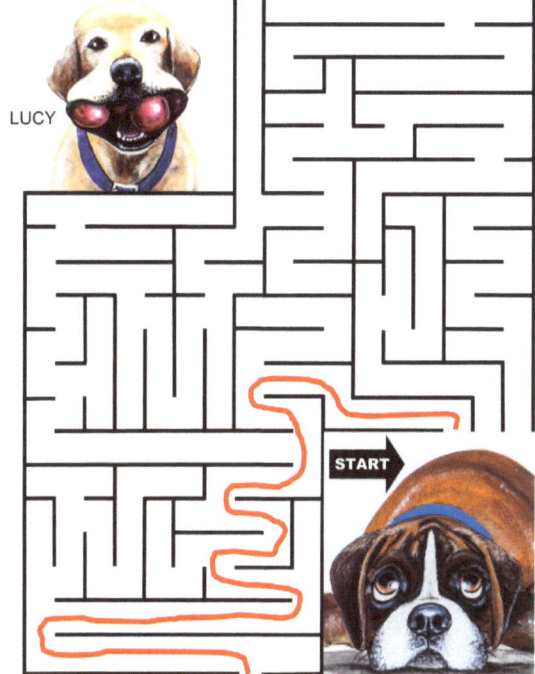

LUCY

START

There are always other options when our way is blocked. Who can Benson now connect with when he feels lonely?

ANSWER PAGE
BRAIN MAZE

Benson's fear meant he stopped doing the things he used to enjoy. Doing nothing and going nowhere, because we are afraid, means we are trapped. It is like being lost in a **MAZE** and not knowing the way out!

INSTRUCTIONS: Make your way through the BRAIN MAZE to find out what helped Benson move forward.

CAUTION! You will need to navigate your way around Amy G'dala. Amy and her twin sister are always on the alert, sensing every danger. Be brave and keep going!

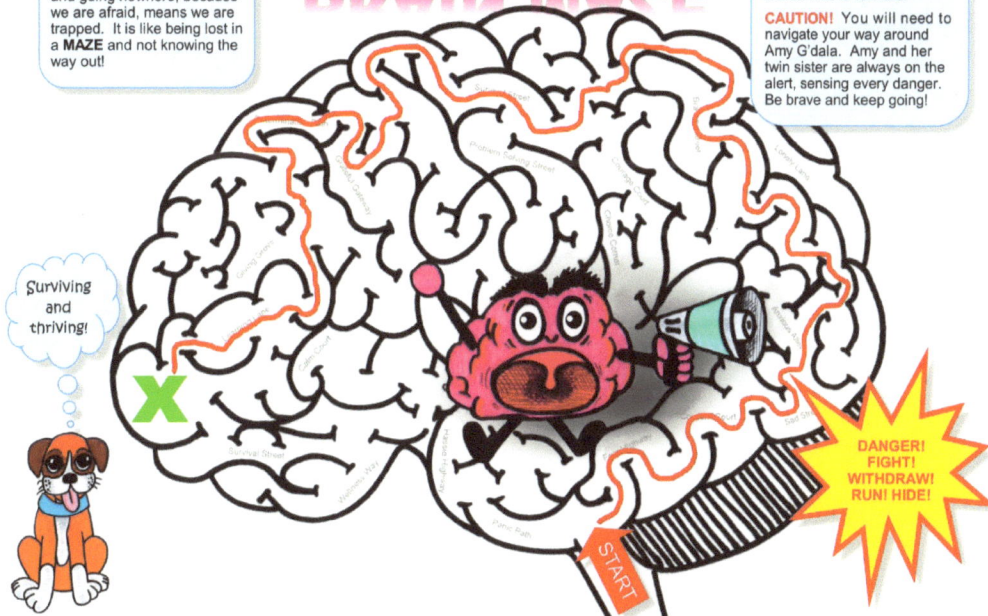

Surviving and thriving!

X

DANGER! FIGHT! WITHDRAW! RUN! HIDE!

START

Author: Karen J Ferry

Karen is in private practice as a Neuropsychotherapist. She holds degrees in Education, a Master's Degree in Counselling (University of Queensland) and is a certified Clinical Neuropsychotherapy Practitioner. Karen has also been an educator for over 35 years and has experience in primary and secondary classrooms, and has worked with families in home education environments. She now specializes in counselling students who have suffered situations of loss, and those facing difficulties at home or school, offering neuropsychotherapy strategies to nurture, empower and move a child forward from difficult or traumatic situations.

www.brainsmarteducation.com

Illustrator: Selinah Bull

Australian artist Selinah Bull creates original works that span multiple media. From personal artworks to fine art photography, each piece is created with love and attention to detail. Selinah has loved art and design for as long as she can remember and she especially enjoys creating fun, imaginative and whimsical paintings for children. Her inspiration comes from being able to touch people's lives with her artworks. Selinah lives and works on the Far North Coast of NSW, Australia.

www.selinahbull.com